Stan Grant is a Wiradjuri and Kamilaroi man. A journalist since 1987, he has worked for the ABC, SBS, the Seven Network and Sky News Australia. From 2001 to 2012 he worked for CNN as an anchor and senior correspondent in Asia and the Middle East. As a journalist, he has received a string of prestigious international and Australian awards. In 2015, he published his bestselling book *Talking to My Country*, which won the Walkley Book Award, and he also won a Walkley Award for his coverage of Indigenous affairs. In 2016 he was appointed to the Referendum Council on Indigenous recognition. Stan is now Professor of Global Affairs at Griffith University and International Affairs Analyst at ABC.

Also by Stan Grant

The Tears of Strangers
Talking to My Country

STAN GRANT

AUSTRALIA DAY

HarperCollins*Publishers*

HarperCollins*Publishers*

Australia • Brazil • Canada • France • Germany • Holland • Hungary
India • Italy • Japan • Mexico • New Zealand • Poland • Spain • Sweden
Switzerland • United Kingdom • United States of America

First published in Australia in 2019
This edition published in 2021
by HarperCollins*Publishers* Australia Pty Limited
ABN 36 009 913 517
harpercollins.com.au

A catalogue record for this book is available from the National Library of Australia

ISBN 978 1 4607 5997 4 (paperback)
ISBN 978 1 4607 0780 7 (ebook)
ISBN 978 1 4607 9792 1 (audio)

Cover design by Darren Holt, HarperCollins Design Studio
Cover images: Map showing the distribution of Aboriginal tribes of Australia
by Norman B. Tindale, courtesy State Library of Queensland. (Record number:
21124881560002061)
Typeset in Minion Pro Regular by Kirby Jones
Author photo: Kathy Luu
Printed and bound in Australia by McPherson's Printing Group
The papers used by HarperCollins in the manufacture of this book are a natural,
recyclable product made from wood grown in sustainable plantation forests. The fibre
source and manufacturing processes meet recognised international environmental
standards, and carry certification.

To Lowanna, John, Dylan, Jesse – my children.
This country and this world are yours.

I say we have a bitter heritage,
but that is not to run it down.

Randolph Stow, *Tourmaline*

CONTENTS

AUTHOR'S NOTE

In 2016 I took my youngest son through the law: the *burrbang*. That is what my Wiradjuri ancestors called initiation – a coming of age when a boy would leave childhood to become a man. Once my son's body would have been ritually scarred as old men unlocked ancient secrets. But I took him on another journey – a journey into the secrets of Australia. I told him stories that we don't tell – stories of the *Great Australian Silence*. We took a road trip back to the country of my ancestors, we passed its fields, its rocks, its rivers and streams. I had been away from Australia for many years. It was a refuge I suppose, I needed to breathe – this place can bear down hard. But now I was home, with my son, and I needed answers to questions that I had carried with me for a lifetime.

That journey became a book, *Talking to My Country*. I wrote it as Australia was again torn apart by race. Each week football fans booed and hounded the Indigenous AFL player, Adam Goodes, until he walked away from a game he had loved. I wanted to tell Australia how this country could make us feel; how it could lay us so low. As I wrote then, Australia's 'wounds rest deep and uneasily in our soul. I am the sum of many things, but I am all history'.

In the years since I have wondered about that: is that true – am I bound forever to my history? Is this my son's inheritance? This is what I try to answer now. This book is my attempt to break free. What is it to be Australian? I look at land, family, race, history and nation – five things that go to my identity. This book is drawn from a collection of speeches and essays – particularly the *Quarterly Essay* 'The Australian Dream: Blood, History and Becoming', published by Black Inc. – but I have taken the licence to play around with them, join the dots and clarify some of my thoughts. Together they are a window onto my country and myself. These past years I have changed and my country has changed – but I ask that same question: who are we?

AUSTRALIA

DAY

INTRODUCTION

I am Australian. There is no other place on earth from where I could come. Think about that: I could only have been created here. The history of this land runs through my veins. I am old and I am new. My bloodline connects me to the first footprints on this continent. Two million sunrises have put me here.

My name – Grant – was shipped here in chains. John Grant, an Irish rebel – just a boy really – banished forever from his home, transported to this penal colony. He would never touch the soil of Tipperary again; he lies in a field under a headstone in the rich plains west of the Blue Mountains in New South Wales.

He left behind a new family: not just Aboriginal and no longer Irish, but something entirely new. We imagine that history rises and falls; we mark time by beginnings and endings. The arrival of Europeans on these shores was not the end for my Aboriginal ancestors or I wouldn't be here. I also carry Ireland deep in me, enough to feel I'd come home when I first walked the streets of Belfast. That's how history works; we don't move in straight lines, we weave in and out of each other. We sail our ships and find new worlds. As novelist Richard Flanagan says, 'We – our histories, our souls – are ... in a process of constant decomposition and reinvention.' This is becoming; this is what we do, humans. We are on a never-ending journey towards each other. We are strangers and then we are family. Before we even called this place Australia, an Australian family – my family – was born.

This is my history. It lives in me.

Australia is the name we give this place, but what is in a name? Nothing really ... and yet everything. People have died for this place we name Australia. This is what we have built, all of us, and it is precious. It exists in us. We carry it in our stories. That's what matters: story. A nation is nothing if not a story: memories and history.

I am Australian. I have Australian memories: sun-scorched days at the pool; sticky orange ice blocks; backyard cricket; broken bicycle chains; hot chips and vinegar; warm milk at recess; inkwells; wet woollen jumpers; frost-cracked fingers.

I am Australian. I have Australian history: Captain Cook; the First Fleet; convicts; Blaxland, Lawson and Wentworth; Burke and Wills; Merino sheep; the Gold Rush; Gallipoli; the Great Depression; Menzies and Gough.

I am Australian and I have other memories. Australian memories: a dirt road on the outskirts of town; mangy dogs and broken glass; my father's wounds; my mother's poems of stolen kids and welfare men; too many funerals.

I am Australian and I have another history. An Australian history: Bennelong, Pemulwuy and Windradyne, who met the British on the frontier, fought, forged friendships, made peace; Truganini and the black line in Tasmania; the Appin massacre; martial law in Bathurst; segregated missions; the Day of Mourning; no blacks allowed and the Freedom Ride.

This is me. All of it. We are all of this. It just is.

But then, it isn't. Now it feels like a battleground. It is as if this day – Australia Day – must pit my ancestors white and black in some conflict without end. It is a fight with myself; I can't possibly win. What am I supposed to forget? What part of my story am I expected to embrace and what part do I reject?

In *A Poison Tree,* William Blake wrote:

I was angry with my friend;
I told my wrath, my wrath did end.
I was angry with my foe:
I told it not, my wrath did grow.

I wonder, would he write those words today? What would Blake think of social media, where our voices are amplified, yet our anger grows. What was meant to bring us together is more often a star chamber where people are put on trial by nameless, faceless trolls. It has become a battleground for ever more strident identities.

We prize identity more than citizenship. We look to what divides us; define ourselves in opposition to each other. This is an age of grievance, and grievance is a demoralising basis for identity. It is a contest of wounds; a contest in which there can be no winner. Wounds are trumps. At its worst, these singular identities tear the world apart. This is the world I have seen; a world that straddles dangerous fault lines of race, history, religion, ideology. We never learn, it is like we are hardwired for this; we form our tribes and we go to war.

Today, we call this the politics of identity and it is among the great perils of our time. This is identity that breeds in the swamplands of history; history as betrayal; a narrative of loss and inheritance robbed. It is history told from the losing end. It is feeding the resurgence of global populism, from Donald Trump's 'Make America Great Again' to Vladimir Putin's lament for the Soviet empire or Xi Jinping's reminder to the Chinese people of the hundred years of humiliation by foreign powers; and it laps against our shores too.

It has been said that looking at history takes one's breath away. I admit to the choking feeling of living with the burden of the past. As an Indigenous Australian I have felt torn between embracing and celebrating all that is great in our nation, living with the all too painful reality that it is not so great for everyone; and that my family, like so many other Indigenous families, has paid a terrible price for the greatness of Australia. For too long the worst of our history was denied or silenced. But no longer. As uncomfortable as it is, we are reckoning with our history. On 26 January, no Australian can really look away.

As a nation we must ask hard questions of ourselves and there is something that gnaws at me. Yes, it is important to remember, but do we also have to let go? Is forgetting the price we must pay for peace? The history of the world is conquest and violence, nations are born in blood: revolution and war. No land is ever surrendered, but can those vanquished ever win justice? Is reconciliation the best that we can hope for? We write anthems to nations, yet we are still to find a song we can all sing. We must ask ourselves difficult questions on Australia Day. What does it mean to call ourselves a nation? As the nineteenth-century French historian Ernest Renan wrote, a nation is a 'daily referendum'; he meant that a nation is never finished, that whatever our differences there is a collective will to live together. There are those who want the date changed from 26 January, others who wish to keep it and some who want Australia Day abolished entirely.

Shouldn't we first ask: who are we? The debate around our national day tests our democracy: a moral and political claim by a minority that challenges the very legitimacy and morality of the majority. Can we celebrate a day that marks the extraordinary achievements of our nation, when others see it as an insult? Whether the day is moved or not, still we must live together.

These past years, I have travelled back into our past, untangling the crooked branches of my family tree, how they wind around each other – black and white. All of our families are planted in this soil, together we are a creole garden that we call a nation. As a boy I loved trees, I loved climbing them to escape from the world. For hours I would hide out in the big old gumtree at the back of my grandmother's house. If anyone called for me I would stay silent, hoping to grab just a little more time on my own. I could think there and what I thought about most were those people I called my own, I thought about what put us here and I thought about getting away.

Even then, a boy of eleven or twelve, I knew there beat in me a fierce contest for my soul. Later I would realise this was not at all unusual. I read the African-American philosopher W.E.B. Du Bois, and he felt the same 'double consciousness'; within him, he said, beat the soul of an American and the soul of an African. Dr Du Bois looked at America and called it out. Could it live up to its creed of equality? Could it rise above its original sin of slavery? Du Bois turned to history's greatest thinkers, he immersed himself in the ideas of liberalism that emerged from the seventeenth and eighteenth centuries. It was the age of reason, the Enlightenment, that set loose in the world the promise of liberty and freedom. The idea of America would have been impossible without the Enlightenment. Yet, Du Bois knew that the founding fathers had betrayed their own faith.

There is in me, too, a deep Aboriginal spirit and the yearning to be Australian – and I don't wish to deny or lose either. Can I live in the Enlightenment *and* the Dreaming? Can I be black *and* white? Can liberal democracy, Australia's founding faith – the promise of equality and justice – truly work for us all? Du Bois famously said that the problem of the twentieth century would be the 'problem of the colour line'; that problem has carried over with me into the twenty-first century and like that little boy in the tree I wonder if I will ever escape it.

If there is one promise of the Enlightenment, it is this: the hope of what one of its foundational thinkers, Immanuel Kant, called 'perpetual peace'. Kant said we must put away 'the ball and chain of permanent, everlasting, minority'; we must imagine ourselves beyond our tribes. To be tied to tribe or nation is to remain tied to the ball and chain of childhood. We would find peace when we saw ourselves in each other. It is a glorious idea, that I can be liberated from race or culture; but it is an idea whose time is yet to come. Perhaps it is beyond us. We don't stray too far from the clan; the light of the cave draws us back and the light of a distant hill is to be feared. History reminds us time and again how we are hardwired to make war against each other.

Yet, I believe that liberalism *is* our best chance; our shot at the 'end of history', that moment when we can put aside the things that divide us. I do not have to be a prisoner of my past or a captive of my race; I can open my life to the possibilities of the world. If there is such a thing as a cosmopolitan – *a citizen of everywhere* – it is me.

Still I am drawn back here; to this *somewhere*. No matter where I go, I can only truly belong here. Australia is my home and it is my battleground; the place where I confront my own tribe. We are each other. In my case, it is physical: I am a part of you as you are a part of me.

At a time when we yell from the fringes I look to the words of the great philosopher of liberty, John Stuart Mill, who looked for the elusive centre, 'softening their extreme forms, and filling up the intervals between them'. I am the conquered and the conqueror, the coloniser and the colonised, black and white – and somewhere among all of that contradiction is an Australian and if I cannot be an Australian I am not sure I can really be anything.

THE VIEW FROM
THE SHORE

In 2018 Australia Day turned angrier. There was spit in the air; clenched fists and tens of thousands of voices raised in what sounded like a collective snarl. Momentum had been growing to change the date; now it was approaching a tipping point. Some Australian local councils had already abandoned the celebration. Everything was up for grabs: our history, our monuments and statues, our flag. The twenty-sixth of January was now a battleground in a culture war over just what it was to be an Australian. Indeed, some of the Aboriginal protesters maintained they were not Australian at all but something else, something rooted in an ancient sovereignty never ceded. The landing of the First Fleet in 1788 did nothing to change that. What were once called tribes are now reconstituted as nations. It is a resurgence of black pride: languages almost dead are being revived; some people are reclaiming traditional names. This Australia Day was a battle over nationhood: who defined it and who belonged. The mood was captured in the acronym of the activist group Warriors of the Aboriginal Resistance – WAR. Old political hardheads were reborn, like pied pipers leading a new generation of activists; they mounted podiums and seized microphones, rallying the crowds like it was 1970 again.

The biggest protest was in Melbourne, at least 60,000 people. They chanted, 'Always was, always will be Aboriginal land'; they carried banners calling for 'Justice', proclaiming a 'day of mourning'. Onlookers celebrating, proudly waving the Australian flag, were told they should be ashamed of themselves. One protester screamed, 'If you celebrate Australia Day, fucker, you're celebrating the death of my ancestors.' One of the activists, a well-known writer who identifies as Indigenous, said Australia did not deserve a day of national celebration in any capacity. Someone else was more blunt: 'Fuck Australia, hope it burns to the ground.'

I knew where this anger came from; I had felt it myself. At a younger age I may well have been among them. I had cursed Australia, I felt no allegiance to a country that had rejected me. As I had written in my book *Talking to my Country*, 'Australia was for other people'. Australia was white. It has been a long road to becoming an Australian, first I had to leave. It was overseas that I realised just how Australian I was; all of those clichés are true: we don't stand on ceremony, we are quick to laugh and we laugh loudly, we work hard and we treat people as we find them. Wherever I moved I would keep an ear open for that familiar accent. I realised for the first time, we *are* a people – black and white; two centuries together on a harsh isolated continent has changed us.

Now, on 26 January 2018, I was far from home again, in another part of the world, and on this day, I was glad of it. I watched the protests on the television news in my hotel room. The Australian Chamber of Commerce had invited me to Hong Kong to give the annual Australia Day address. It is funny that I

say 'far from home', because in so many ways Hong Kong is home
to me. I lived there for several years, working for the American
broadcasting giant CNN. This teeming former Chinese outpost
of the British Empire is special to me. The years my family spent
there were professionally and personally among the happiest of
my life. Hong Kong was where we truly became a family, where
we bonded most tight.

When we had touched down the night before, all was right
with the world. I always felt that way coming in to land, looking
down at the water and the jagged coastlines of the dotted islands
below. My wife and I caught the airport train into Hong Kong
central and then a taxi to our hotel. We always laughed to
ourselves in a Hong Kong cab, at how the driver could accelerate
and brake seemingly at the same time; giving the car a lurching,
surging quality. We hovered between whiplash and motion
sickness, but it was one of the rituals of being back and it gave me
comfort that some things never change.

I wanted to overdose on Hong Kong, I wanted to breathe it all
in, not waste a minute. It had been a few years since we had been
back, and I was eager to taste it all again. There was a little hole-
in-the-wall roast pork restaurant just around the corner from
where we used to go for Buddhist meditation classes. There it
was, exactly as I remembered it, the same crispy skin pork
hanging in the window. Wan Chai, a busy bar strip area, was
humming and we pushed our way through the crowds spilling
out of the clubs and pubs. I could hear the Filipino bands and see
the girls on the street luring half-drunk red-faced white men in
for another drink. If we ate quickly enough, my wife and I could
get a cab to the other end of the island to our old favourite foot
massage place. Home is always about the small things. As an

Aboriginal person I am meant to talk about my spiritual connection to my country and it is true I do feel that intensely, but Hong Kong – in its own way and for different reasons – speaks just as powerfully to my soul.

Australia looks different from afar. I spent nearly two decades away from my homeland, living in London, Hong Kong, Beijing, Abu Dhabi, Dubai. To me it was liberating. I could breathe. I didn't have to fight old battles, I wasn't braced for the next stupid remark, moment of ignorance or just plain racism. Other Indigenous people have said the same thing: so this is what freedom feels like. It feels good. It feels like being a person, a human being in my own right, not a product of history or a projection of identity. Australia is tiring; I always felt the adrenalin of survival was slowly wearing me down. Don't think for a moment I was somehow immune; yes, I was what most people would judge successful, I had an interesting career, was financially comfortable, but Australia could still lay me low. Too many people in my family died young, too many had their ambitions denied, too many locked away, too many lost to drugs or alcohol. I know what put them there: they were born into it; born into a history hung like a dead weight over their lives. Success had bought me distance; I could escape but not truly be free.

Now, I watched these scenes playing out on television as I prepared to speak on this day – a world away, yes, but Australia Day still – a day that those I would claim as my own called a day of invasion.

You can call it what you want
but it just don't mean a thing

I had punched the air and sung along with the song by A.B. Original. Their hit 'January 26', touched something deep in me. It was a witty, brutal put-down of flag-waving Aussie jingoism. I have always winced at overt displays of patriotism; flags and face paint often barely obscuring a deeper menace. Knowing what we know, knowing how this country was taken, knowing what became of a people who had lived here for 65,000 years at least, knowing about children taken from their families, about people segregated, about deaths in cells; knowing all of that, waving a flag seemed like mockery, like the final insult.

And yet … and yet. What disturbed me so? Yes, A.B. Original spoke to my heart but my head said something else. My head was unconvinced by this strident rejection of Australia. Who made that song a hit? Who paid for it and played it loud? Australians. Yes, those same Australians lampooned and sneered at: 'Fuck that, homie'. Yes, those Australians: they were prepared to look at themselves and question their history. They marched for reconciliation and protested about injustice. Those Australians, were they to be condemned? Those Australians whose taxes funded programs to better educate Indigenous kids, to improve health, to build houses: billions of dollars a year. Did I hope their Australia burned to the ground? No.

In Hong Kong we caught up with dear friends. Our children had grown up together, we had spent hours at the beach together, we had shared Christmases and birthdays and countless dinners. We were bonded as expats in a foreign land, but we were also bonded as Australians. We shared the same accent, we knew the same TV shows, we sang the same songs, we knew what it was like to fill the days of a long hot Aussie summer holiday. We knew caravan parks and the outback and public pools. Did it matter that I was Aboriginal and they were white? Not in the least. To be honest we rarely talked about it. We talked politics and history and we swapped books and shared ideas and laughed. They were Australian and I was Australian. In Hong Kong, a long way from home, in our new home, being Australian was just a lot easier. Would I hope that their Australia burned to the ground? No.

Forget for a minute that I am an Aboriginal person. How would this look to me, these protesters, damning Australia to hell? Australia is a paradise, so many people have told me that. So had the years I spent working in the hellholes of the world, reporting on victims of circumstance, from the refugees in camps in war-torn Afghanistan, to the weeping mothers at terrorist bombings, to children blinded by trachoma in remote villages in China, to the hunched-over, malnourished, vacant-eyed farmers I gazed at from my slow train across North Korea – any one of them would have risked everything for a shot at a new life in Australia. Should their dream of Australia be burned to the ground? No.

Watching the protests on my television, I can't help but see them through different eyes. The fact that people are free to protest at all is remarkable. Ours is a country where we have the right to take to the streets – to burn our flag if we wish. I had spent the best part of a decade reporting in China, where protests like this would be shut down. I had reported from Baghdad and Kabul and Islamabad where a public gathering like this could easily end in disaster, a suicide bomb tearing people limb from limb. Here, the police cleared the path and kept the peace. For all of the vitriol, there would be no violence. This is how democracy works; we have the right to shake a fist at power. Societies like ours are no accident. They are hard earned. We build nations like ours on sweat and trust. I have seen countries lurch into revolution, I have seen democracy subverted by coups and uniformed strongmen claim power at the barrel of a gun. I wonder, do the protesters on this day realise that they are railing against a country whose people had fought and died in foreign wars for freedoms just like this. Do they want this Australia to burn to the ground?

This Australia, the Australia of my friends, the Australia of my birth, the Australia that held our stories, our history, our laws: this was my Australia as much as anyone's. This Australia, that shone like a beacon for those around the world seeking a new beginning: this was my Australia too. Australia did look different from afar. It had always left its mark on me; its hills, its rivers, its plains, its valleys and deserts had all shaped me. When I thought of home that is what I pictured. But I had sought escape from another Australia, an Australia that had shut me out. This was an Australia whose constitution was written so that we did not count. I had lived between the Australia of my head and the Australia of my heart. Australia did look different from afar. The years away had changed me and changed how I saw my country. I looked at it with new eyes. Now I was watching, again from far away as people – my people – hoped that it would burn to the ground.

What I was seeing was really bigger than Australia; bigger than the struggle of Indigenous people. This was another front in a *global* battle for recognition; a desire for people to be heard; to be seen. It has uprooted politics as we know it: it is a scream from the fringes; a blowback against what we are told is the modern world; a globalised future of universal values, free trade and open borders.

This was the promise of the End of History, Francis Fukuyama's bold phrase for the post-Cold War world where liberal democracy reigned supreme. But Fukuyama, an American political scientist, had also warned of a 'nostalgia for the time when history existed'. History indeed is back. Nationalism, tribalism, sectarianism: we walk dangerous fault lines. Everywhere there are demagogues and populists, feeding on anxiety, fear, racism and xenophobia. They are the most successful politicians of our time and they understand one essential thing: identity matters. That was what I was seeing, this was identity. A people told they were doomed for extinction; for whom the dying pillow was being smoothed, now saying, 'We are here and we won't be silenced.'

*

I remember another Australia Day, just two years earlier. I had been in Washington, DC, reporting on then prime minister Malcolm Turnbull's meeting with Barack Obama. Now I was preparing to fly out, the weather forecasters telling me that Washington would soon be snowed in. This was a blizzard of record proportions. The capital was buried under two feet of snow. The mid-Atlantic states of the US had rarely seen anything like it. Television networks were covering the impact around the clock; it was now rated category 4, or a 'crippling storm'. More than fifty people would be killed and thousands left without power or stranded. I made it out just hours before the airport was shut down. In Australia it was already tomorrow.

Just the day before, I had stood in the Oval Office at the White House, almost close enough to reach out and touch the president of the United States. This was familiar territory for me and I was in my element. I relished the long hours and irregular meals, the sleeplessness and constant anxiety of life on the road. The freezing temperatures only added to the excitement. My cameraman and I were working from 7 a.m. to 4 a.m. the following day. This was the curse of the international dateline: night was day and day was night; we were always on deadline. The snow was coming down in sheets so heavy that at times I would vanish from the television screen, a voice lost in a blizzard.

The prime minister and the president were focused on China, the great foreign policy puzzle of our age. More than anything else – terrorism, Russia, economic crisis – the relationship between the superpower and its emerging rival will likely determine the course of the twenty-first century. Were the two countries on a collision course that would plunge the world into conflict? Certainly China, rich and powerful, is making its presence felt, challenging American hegemony. The flashpoints stretch from the 'Sea of Japan', to the South China Sea; from the North Korean border to disputed Kashmir, where China faces an old and equally rising foe in India.

Malcolm Turnbull had recently spoken of the 'Thucydides Trap': a warning from the Peloponnesian war that a rising Athens made conflict with Sparta inevitable. Now China and the US were in danger of repeating history. Before leaving Washington, I and other reporters quizzed the prime minister at a reception held at the home of the departing Australian Ambassador to the US, Kim Beazley.

World leaders, global events; it was a long way to come for a boy who had lived much of his early life on the road, as my family moved from town to town searching for work. We were poor, essentially homeless, relying on whatever food my father's muscles would provide, and when that failed, whatever the churches or charities would give us. We were not just poor, we were black – Aborigines – or, as we were more likely to be called then, 'Abos'. Now here I was flying from Washington to Sydney, clutching a book recounting the Obama presidency, relieved I had escaped the blizzard but, unbeknownst to me, about to fly into a different kind of storm. A speech I had given months earlier and promptly forgotten had suddenly 'gone viral'.

In 2015 I had been invited by the Ethics Centre in Sydney to participate in a debate on whether 'Racism is Destroying the Australian Dream'. For the longest time I had said no. It was a heated time in Australia; the Indigenous Australian Rules footballer Adam Goodes had been booed out of the game. For weeks on end he endured this chorus of derision from opposing fans. It wasn't just booing a sportsman, this was something else: it came from deep inside us, from that wound in Australia that had never healed. Adam was a hero, a two-time winner of the game's highest honour, the Brownlow Medal. He was considered one of the greatest players of his generation. But he was more than that. Adam had become a powerful voice for reconciliation; he devoted his life to trying to bring black and white together in Australia. In 2014, Adam Goodes was Australian of the Year.

But all of that turned on a day when he heard a word from the crowd. Someone had called him an ape; he turned and saw a young girl and demanded she be evicted from the ground. He had heard it too many times before; it was the taunt of the schoolyard, the insult that rang in his ears as his family moved from small town to small town. He thought – he had hoped – he was now free of that. But now, here it was again and from a young girl. Why would she say it? What bigotry or racism had shaped her? He would seek to understand that later. He would reach out to the girl, talk to her. But now he just felt anger and shame and pain. He wanted her gone. From that moment on he was a conduit for all of the pent-up anger, guilt, shame and blame in our country. To some he had crossed a line; he was no longer a sportsman, he had brought politics onto the football field. It was an unforgivable sin; a line that can't be crossed. The back page was now front page and Adam Goodes became a symbol for a nation still struggling with its past.

I wrote an article for *The Guardian* newspaper, trying to bridge the divide. I didn't want to vilify people for booing Goodes, I wanted to tell Australia how it made me feel; how it made us feel as Indigenous people. As I wrote, what we heard was not a boo, but a howl; a howl of humiliation that echoed across two centuries of injustice and exclusion. We were estranged, I said, in the land of our ancestors. But I clung to something more; I clung to the hope that for all of that we were a nation better than its worst. I clung to a hope that out of the torment of this Aboriginal man, out of the pain of Adam Goodes, we might find a new faith in ourselves.

In that one article, a thousand words or so, my life changed. I was no longer simply a journalist, someone who observed the world and wrote the stories of others, I was at the centre of a story of me, my people, my country; a story as old as this continent. The impact of that article meant what I said now mattered. I was asked to write, I was asked to give speeches, I was invited to schools and conferences. Australians wanted to hear this story and for many reasons – the moment, the time – they wanted to hear it from me. It is an unnerving thing to find your ideas, your words, are bigger than you. What I had to say was more important than who I was. I wasn't sure I wanted this. I knew I wasn't entirely worthy of it and that there were those with more important things to say.

When the Ethics Centre first invited me to the debate, I declined. I'm still not completely sure why I relented; they persisted and I probably ran out of excuses not to do it. I know when I took that stage I wanted to speak from my heart. I wanted to speak unrehearsed and unscripted. I wanted it to be immediate and forceful. I wanted to look the audience in the eye and hold them. I carried in my pocket something that connected me to where I was from; to my ancestors and to my country. In the weeks leading up to the debate I received a letter from an old man from Cowra in western New South Wales. He had grown up on a property that had been the traditional home of my Wiradjuri forebears. As a boy he had collected artefacts, then still scattered on the ground. He had lost them all save one, a perfectly formed stone axe. He said he didn't feel as though it belonged to him and wanted to return it to me. It was a powerful gesture that spoke of who we are in this country, of how this land is our land – all of us. This stone axe from my ancestors, through the hands of an old farmer to me, connected us to an unbroken story. As much as anything it shaped what I wished to say that night.

I didn't want to look away at notes. I didn't need them for this story, which I had been told since childhood. It was a story I had reported on as a journalist in faraway countries; stories of other peoples who had felt the sting of invasion and colonisation. It was a 'war story', and as the Vietnamese-American writer and academic Viet Thanh Nguyen, speaking of his own turbulent history, says, 'All wars are fought twice, the first time on the battlefield, the second time in memory.'

*

27 October 2015: City Recital Hall, Sydney, New South Wales

Thank you so much for coming along this evening and I would also like to extend my respects to my Gadigal brothers and sisters from my people, the Wiradjuri people.

In the winter of 2015, Australia turned to face itself. It looked into its soul and it had to ask this question: who are we? What sort of country do we want to be? And this happened in a place that is most holy, most sacred to Australians. It happened on the sporting field, it happened on the football field. Suddenly the front page was on the back page, it was in the grandstands.

Thousands of voices rose to hound an Indigenous man. A man who was told he wasn't Australian. A man who was told he wasn't Australian of the Year. And they hounded that man into submission.

I can't speak for what lay in the hearts of the people who booed Adam Goodes. But I can tell you what we heard when we heard those boos. We heard a sound that was very familiar to us.

We heard a howl. We heard a howl of humiliation that echoes across two centuries of dispossession, injustice, suffering and survival. We heard the howl of the Australian Dream and it said to us again, you're not welcome.

The Australian Dream.

We sing of it, and we recite it in verse:

Australians all, let us rejoice for we are young and free.

My people die young in this country. We die ten years

younger than average Australians and we are far from free.
We are fewer than three per cent of the Australian
population and yet we are twenty-five per cent, a quarter, of
those Australians locked up in our prisons – and if you are a
juvenile, it is worse, it is fifty per cent. An Indigenous child
is more likely to be locked up in prison than they are to
finish high school.

I love a sunburned country, a land of sweeping plains, of
rugged mountain ranges …

It reminds me that my people were killed on those
plains. We were shot on those plains, disease ravaged us on
those plains.

I come from those plains. I come from a people west of
the Blue Mountains, the Wiradjuri people, where in the
1820s the soldiers and settlers waged a war of extermination
against my people.

Yes, a war of extermination!

That was the language used at the time. Go to the
Sydney Gazette and look it up and read about it. Martial law
was declared and my people could be shot on sight.

Those rugged mountain ranges – my people, women
and children, were herded over those ranges to their deaths.

The Australian Dream.

The Australian Dream is rooted in racism. It is the very
foundation of the dream. It is there at the birth of the
nation. It is there in terra nullius. An empty land. A land for
the taking. Sixty thousand years of occupation. A people
who made the first seafaring journey in the history of
mankind. A people of law, a people of lore, a people of music
and art and dance and politics. None of it mattered because

our rights were extinguished because we were not here according to British law.

And when British people looked at us, they saw something sub-human, and if we were human at all, we occupied the lowest rung on civilisation's ladder. We were fly-blown, stone-age savages and that was the language that was used. Charles Dickens, the great writer of the age, when referring to the noble savage of which we were counted among, said, 'It would be better that they be wiped off the face of the earth.'

Captain Arthur Phillip, a man of enlightenment, a man who was instructed to make peace with the so-called natives in a matter of years, was sending out raiding parties with the instruction, 'Bring back the severed heads of the black troublemakers.'

My people were rounded up and put on missions from where, if you escaped, you were hunted down, you were roped and tied and dragged back, and it happened here. It happened on the mission that my grandmother and my great-grandmother are from, the Warangesda on the Darlington Point of the Murrumbidgee River.

Read about it. It happened.

By 1901 when we became a nation, when we federated the colonies, we were nowhere. We're not in the constitution, save for 'race provisions' which have allowed for laws to be made that would take our children, that would invade our privacy, that would tell us who we could marry and tell us where we could live.

The Australian Dream.

By 1963, the year of my birth, the dispossession was continuing. Police came at gunpoint under cover of

darkness to Mapoon, an Aboriginal community in
Queensland, and they ordered people from their homes and
they burned those homes to the ground and they gave the
land to a bauxite mining company. And today those people
remember that as the 'Night of the Burning'.

In 1963, when I was born, I was counted among the
flora and fauna, not among the citizens of this country.

Now, you will hear things tonight. You will hear people
say, 'But you've done well.' Yes, I have and I'm proud of it,
and why have I done well? I've done well because of who has
come before me. My father, who lost the tips of three fingers
working in sawmills to put food on our table because he was
denied an education. My grandfather, who served to fight
wars for this country when he was not yet a citizen and
came back to a segregated land where he couldn't even share
a drink with his digger mates in the pub because he was
black.

My great-grandfather, who was jailed for speaking his
language to his grandson (my father). Jailed for it! My
grandfather on my mother's side, who married a white
woman, who reached out to Australia, lived on the fringes
of town until the police came, put a gun to his head,
bulldozed his tin humpy and ran over the graves of the
three children he buried there.

That's the Australian Dream.

I have succeeded in spite of the Australian Dream, not
because of it, and I've succeeded because of those people.

You might hear tonight, 'But you have white blood in
you.' And if the white blood in me was here tonight, my
grandmother, she would tell you of how she was turned

away from a hospital giving birth to her first child because
she was giving birth to the child of a black person.

The Australian Dream.

We're better than this. I have seen the worst of the world
as a reporter. I spent a decade in war zones from Iraq to
Afghanistan and Pakistan. We are an extraordinary
country. We are in so many respects the envy of the world.
If I was sitting here where my friends are tonight, I would be
arguing passionately for this country. But I stand here with
my ancestors, and the view looks very different from where
I stand.

The Australian Dream.

We have our heroes. Albert Namatjira painted the soul
of this nation. Vincent Lingiari put his hand out for Gough
Whitlam to pour the sand of his country through his
fingers and say, 'This is my country.' Cathy Freeman lit the
torch of the Olympic Games.

But every time we are lured into the light, we are
mugged by the darkness of this country's history.

Of course racism is destroying the Australian Dream. It
is self-evident that it's destroying the Australian Dream. But
we are better than that.

The people who stood up and supported Adam Goodes
and said, 'No more', they are better than that.

The people who marched across the bridge for
reconciliation, they are better than that.

The people who supported Kevin Rudd when he said
sorry to the Stolen Generations, they are better than that.

My children and their non-Indigenous friends are better
than that. My wife, who is not Indigenous, is better than that.

And one day, I want to stand here and be able to say as
proudly and sing as loudly as anyone else in this room,
Australians all, let us rejoice.

Thank you.

*

The speech was first broadcast as the opening address of a debate,
and attracted little comment, but then, in January 2016, the Ethics
Centre posted the footage on its website. The reaction to and praise
for the speech was – all modesty aside – far more than it deserved.
It was an accident of timing: it coincided with Australia Day, amid
the reflection and celebration, sadness and anger. The broadcaster
and journalist Mike Carlton took to social media to give my speech
an extra push. He called it a 'Martin Luther King moment',
referring to the speeches of the American civil rights leader.

Noel Pearson, the Indigenous lawyer and activist, in an
address to the National Press Club, called my speech a 'tour de
force'. He said it did for black Australia what Prime Minister Paul
Keating's Redfern speech did for white Australia in 1992, when
Keating laid bare Australia's dark history of frontier wars and
stolen children. But the stakes were higher for Keating than for
me. Never before had a prime minister spoken with such force
and clarity about our history; he was taking Australians to the
other side of the frontier. How many times had I heard that old
political adage: there are no votes in blacks. But that speech
changed Australia; his words that day led all the way to Kevin
Rudd's 'sorry' in 2007 and now to me.

Pearson also reminded us that there was nothing in my
speech 'unfamiliar to blackfellas'. He was right. Pearson himself

has spoken powerfully about our history, notably two decades earlier, in a speech to the 1997 Reconciliation Convention in Melbourne:

> It is a troubling business coming to terms with Australian history, both for Aboriginal people and non-Aboriginal people. For our people it is a troubling business because there is the imperative of never allowing anyone to forget the truths of the past but to be able as a community to rise above its demoralising legacy ... but it's also a challenge for non-Aboriginal Australia, a challenge to understand that in the same way that they urge pride in Gallipoli and in Kokoda ... can we as a community and a nation also acknowledge the shameful aspects of that same past.

There is, in fact, a long and distinguished history of courage and oratory among Indigenous people. Jack Patten, the first president of the Aborigines Progressive Association, inaugurated a day of mourning at the Australian Hall on Elizabeth Street in Sydney on Australia Day, 1938:

> On this day the white people are rejoicing, but we, as Aborigines, have no reason to rejoice on Australia's 150th birthday ... this land belonged to our forefathers ... give us the chance! We do not wish to be left behind in Australia's march to progress ... we do not wish to be herded like cattle.

Charles Perkins, Gary Foley, Chicka Dixon, Marcia Langton, Jackie Huggins, Noel Pearson, Michael Mansell and so many

others have demanded to be heard in a country that for so long
did not want to listen. They have argued for the recognition of
Indigenous rights, of title to land and the need for self-
determination. Far from being Martin Luther King, I stood on
the shoulders of generations of giants.

Nevertheless, I have lived these past years with the weight of
those words. My speech seemingly became all things to all
people. Many Indigenous people felt that in telling my family's
story, I had told their own. Other Australians seized on my belief
that we are better than our worst. To some I may have let white
people off the hook; too readily absolved them of their sins. Yet I
believe it is possible to speak to a country's shame and still have
love for that country. I can no more deny the greatness of
Australia as a peaceful, cohesive, prosperous society than my
fellow countrymen and women can deny the legacy of neglect
and bigotry and injustice that traps so many Indigenous brothers
and sisters still.

Those words have sent me on a journey into my country's
past, into the history of my family and what has put me here –
although in truth I have been on this journey my entire life,
always looking out, always wondering, who am I? Why am I here,
now at this time in this place? I have always felt hemmed in
somehow; searching for a freedom in other places yet always
dragging my history along with me. Because that is it, it is history
that I have sought escape from.

This is what happens when you are told you are doomed, that
your existence – who you are – must be erased. It is what leads a
young boy to scrub his skin red raw to remove the stain of colour.
I was not good enough, that was what I was told over and over
again. Why wouldn't I believe it? And the escape was so easy; just

run, deny it all. And I have run far, to more than seventy countries. But always it was there; always lurking in the background; this question of where I belonged. Could I find a home in the only true home I could ever have?

That speech – not even ten minutes out of a lifetime – changed everything. I said more than I realised. Here was my home, somewhere between invasion and settlement, between terra nullius and Mabo, between Federation and the Tent Embassy. Here was the truth, for me at least. I was not one thing or another, I could not claim to be black and not white; being Aboriginal – Wiradjuri, Kamilaroi – did not mean I was not also Australian.

There are those who seek certainty; who divide the world up and take sides. I don't trust certainty; I know that in certainty, ignorance and deceit lie. Give me questions more than answers. Those Indigenous people who crave certainty see in me someone unthreatening, too diplomatic. But if Australians listen to me at all it is because I don't threaten them. I get that. I know that.

Australia has historically had trouble seeing people like me except in its own image. I am known to Australians. I live and work among them and my face is ambiguous enough to blend in; another dark skin in a rainbow nation. But this is who I am. This is the life I have created. I have moved from the fringes to the centre. I don't want to live in a country fractured by its history. I want to share in a sense of the possibilities of our nation. But I don't want to live in a country that shrouds its past in silence. I don't want to live in a country where the people who share my heritage, whose ancestry connects to the first footprints on our continent, too often live in misery.

To me the most important line in my speech was the last: 'And one day, I want to stand here and be able to say as proudly and sing as loudly as anyone else in this room, Australians all, let us rejoice.'

*

Now, in 2018, here I was in Hong Kong, on another Australia Day, preparing to give another speech while back home other Indigenous people were marching in anger. I felt like I was at war with myself. How can the souls of my ancestors' rest when our national day is a day of shame? Should we change the date from 26 January? That has never seemed to me the right question. Instead, we should be asking: Why should Australia Day be moved? What is it about this day? What does it tell us about ourselves? Can we so easily deny a day that forever altered the story of this land?

The British fleet came, and it brought human cargo and a new tradition; it brought democracy; new laws and new ways of seeing the world. It came at the pinnacle of empire. It came with Enlightenment. The view from the ship was of a new land for a new beginning; a colony that would become a nation. For some this land was a prison from which they would never escape but would in time call home. My story begins on that ship.

The view from shore was of strangers. They had come before and then departed. Now they were back; land would be cleared, buildings erected; this time they were here to stay. They spoke a different language, their bodies were fully clothed, they brought the whip and they brought alcohol. Soon would come disease and violence. In a few short years so many of those on the shore would be gone. The population of the local people was ravaged. In time the survivors would take on new names, their skin would become lighter, they would lose their language for English. My story begins on that shore.

The story of Australia begins on that shore, when a people of steam and steel met a people of flint and bone and wood. A people of Enlightenment met a people of Dreaming. They danced, briefly, on that shore. It is a long-overlooked moment of Australian history, but in those first few months they danced hand in hand on the beach, swapping songs under the moonlight. It is a story told by the late historian, Inga Clendinnen, in her book *Dancing with Strangers*; how these two peoples 'took each other hand in hand like children at a picnic'. Soon the frontier wars would ignite: the years of killing would begin. Between the dance and the destruction is the Australian dream. It is here I find myself. I live between the dance and the destruction. I live between the ship and the shore. It is here that the dream remains unrealised. In this troubled space we all live our lives.

WOZBRA
UDJANINJIN
QUIDJI
WOLJAMIDI
MIRIWUN
NGARINMAN
KWARAN
WALADJADARI
DJERAK
MANDJURA
LUNGA
GIDJA
GIRRI
NORTHERN A
MUDBARA
BILGODJUMNA
TJIN
MADALA
WARWA
MONSAAND
DJARU
WAR
WULUMARI
JULBRE
BUNA:RA
GOODA
WAIADARA
WIMIALA
WALPARI
K
DALIA
CENTRAL
NMATJE
BEDEDO
PINTUBI
JU MU
ARA
KUKATJA
(WES
DJ:DADJARA
PIT JANDJARA
NANDA
ANTAKIR
S RALIA
MANDJINDJA
SO
KADJARA
NADATADJARA
D'ALEA
A:LJEN
WODGA:I
KO
TJERARIDJA:L MURUNITJA
A U S T
OGA:
MIRNID
WIRA
DADJUMMA
A U S T R A L I A N B

PART 1
HOME

THE VANISHING PLACE

I know a place where Australia disappears: it vanishes. Yes, the vanishing place; that's what this is. A place where we go and don't come back. It scares us, this place. It mocks us. We think we have tamed this country with our cities and our towns; our roads and train tracks. We farm it and fence it. Sometimes, I think all we do is lock ourselves in to keep it out. 'I love a sunburned country; a land of sweeping plains.' Do we? Really? We love the idea of it, but the truth is if we get too close it's as though we can't breathe; we seem to get our oxygen from each other. We squeeze ourselves into the tightest spaces, and suck in car fumes. That's what we do in terra nullius – in emptiness – we build things and call them ours. Carl Jung once said, 'land assimilates its conqueror'; it certainly changes us; in time we become part of it. But here in the vanishing place it is eternity I feel, not belonging. This place reminds me of our impermanence. Two hundred years, 65,000 years: this place was here before us and will remain after. We can call this place home but it remains just out of reach. It is a place of mystery. In the vanishing place I feel as though the land itself takes its revenge; this place has the last laugh.

There is a myth about the outback: *beyond here be monsters; if the animals don't get you the blacks will. Out here you die of thirst. Out here you walk for days to go nowhere.*

It is buried deep within us, a myth from the earliest days of the frontier. Out here was danger. Australia? The word itself can't contain all this place is. This place is older than that. I can kick up the dirt here and let thousands of years settle gently all over me. Australia? What is Australia? A map? Lines marking the separation of states and territories? Is it history? Is it our laws? Is it politics? Do we define ourselves by what we have earned? All of this is how we mark time; that's how a land becomes a nation: it is in the stories we tell. But not here. It is just this place. It is this dirt, these trees and rocks. It is a song, sung over and over and over until it seeps into the ground.

In this place, there is no sign; no border; no line in the sand. There is nothing here really that tells us from where we have come, or to point to where we may yet go. In this place there is stillness and silence and forever: forever existing now as it always has.

The stars above me are the stars that have always been here, in a place where time collapses. What was dead is alive: stars long faded whose light lives on, moving through time to brighten my sky. The stars are like the people of this place. They are people long gone, who have left their footprint, whose energy is alive here and now. I can stub my toe on ten thousand years here. A sharpened stone, a piece of charcoal, tell me that this was a living place. It is a living place.

It was a place of story and lore. It was where people fished and hunted and shared the warmth of a campfire. It was where traditions were passed on and over time a collection of people became a culture and society. Our new country, our cities and towns, circle places like this. Just an hour's drive away is a thriving country centre: cinemas and pubs and schools and shops. But here it all falls away. There is nothing to break the flow of people and place.

Nothing. There is nothing here that divides then and now. The measure of time feels futile. The ticking of my watch can mark off the seconds in a day. But what does that matter when the days here bleed seamlessly into each other? Time is a trick. It fools us. There is no time, just what we make of it. I have spoken to the physicist, Carlo Rovelli, about this. Time is a lie, he says, just like the flat earth. There is memory, there is no past. Time passes differently depending on where we are: the higher we are the more quickly does time pass. In a laboratory we can see life at its tiniest: we can see the universe at its most pure and see that it makes no sense. The world of quantum physics is the world of weird science, where things coexist and by mere observation change their shape and nature. At its purest, there is chaos.

Perhaps that's what makes me dizzy here. It is science, it is time, it is memory; there is something in my DNA, something old and something very new that unnerves me. All around me there is openness, not even a fence to hem the horizon. My mind and heartbeat are racing to a rhythm set by the city. Yesterday, I was on a crowded train platform then a plane to bring me here. Now, it seems I have lost my balance: I walk around and around trying to find just the right pace, but I can't settle.

I am here with people who share my own blood. Our family connects us to this place. This is Barkandji, Ngiyampaa and Mutthi Mutthi ancestral country; but it cuts across Wiradjuri country too. My great-grandfather spoke all of these languages; his family was scattered among these other peoples. People for whom we struggle to find words: clan, tribe, nation. None of this fits, just like Australia doesn't fit comfortably within Australia: the Australian story has often been about erasure, about disappearance. And so we mark the ground to give us certainty; state boundaries tell us who we are. Now I am in New South Wales, close to the Victorian border. But I am a world away, lost in the murmur of ancient languages and the embers of old fires and water that no longer flows.

If I am connected here in some way, I am also a stranger. That's what unnerves me the most. I know Australia: Australia the nation, the people. As much as I may sometimes bristle against it, I have some grasp on what it is all the same. But here? There's a thought that doesn't leave me: what is it to belong? Why is it we talk of ownership? I ask one of my cousins: who can say who owns this? I wonder, if the prime minister, leader of this country, was here, what could he point to and say: I rule that. He holds power because a measure of us have put him there and when we take it away he will be stripped bare, just another one of us. But here, there is another power: it isn't the power of nations, it is the power of place.

We have a name for this place, we call it Lake Mungo. Strange, because it ceased to be anything we would recognise as a lake many thousands of years ago. Now, it looks like the surface of the moon: dry and cracked. Life that was here remains buried and fossilised. This is a place of old ceremonies; old rituals; old fires and stories.

There are old bones here, the oldest bones on this continent. Mungo Man, we call him: 42,000 years old, his bones found resting just below the surface in 1974. A rainstorm loosened the earth and there he was. Who knows what else waits to be found in the parched lakebed.

Bones and stones, that's what the old man I am out here with says; bones and stones, that's what people come looking for. He reckons Mungo Man came back to tell us about himself and his people. Mungo Man has been studied and written about, kept for decades in a box in a drawer in a museum, finally returned to his home in 2018. What he has told us has helped connect another link in the chain of human migration that spread from Africa more than a hundred thousand years ago. All of us, set adrift on an open sea on an endless journey to find each other.

There's a dead tree in the distance and a stark, dry branch pokes out at just the right angle. This was once a high-water mark, where I am standing now would have been the shoreline. There are old discarded implements everywhere – stone tools – jagged, sharp rocks honed to a fine point. They would have been used to slit open and scale fresh fish. There are ancient middens and petrified charcoal from long-extinguished fires and all of it just here, all around me – no past, just now – all of it, me and Mungo, here now. I walk over to the tree and nestle into the branch. It is just my size, I can stretch along its length and my head rests where the branch meets the trunk and there I fall asleep: the sleep of tens of thousands of years.

It has that effect, the old man says. He's brought people here before. They cry sometimes, he says; they lie on the ground or sit in the dirt. It is like they want to get as close as they can; to feel it, as though it will tell them something. The old man says, there's too much talk about bones and stones; this is a living place.

Lake Mungo is one of the scary places: the places we – Australians – don't go. These are the places where we disappear. Here, we enter terra nullius, described by academic Elspeth Tilley in her book *White Vanishing*, as the 'disruptive, disturbing, chaotic, uncanny space'. This is fixed in our memory; we tell stories of this: nothing, it seems, rattles us more than those who vanish. I am drawn to something writer Beth Spencer once said, that the Beaumont children, Harold Holt, Azaria Chamberlain, and on and on, inhabit 'this Other space in Australian memory'. There's a suspicion among us that they strayed too far 'off the cultural map and disappeared into thin air'.

This disturbs me too. I feel as though here I too could disappear. It isn't supposed to be like this; I am meant to embrace it all, to reconnect to some severed part of me. Here I am meant to become whole; to be at one with my ancestors. The old man has started to bring boys here to be initiated; put through the law, cut and marked as men. This is renewal: a people reclaiming culture and practice that had long ago ceased. I understand that need to reconnect. I need it too; but there's a thought I can't shake: have I come here looking for certainty, for authenticity or purity? Being Aboriginal is not something I can perform and I cannot pretend that I have an unbroken connection to a deep spiritual past. Being here is like entering what Celtic mythology calls the 'otherworld'; it is a space in-between; the space that makes me who I am.

Out here, in this vanishing place, I know what unbalances me: I am an Australian.

*

Watching the documentary *Palace of Memories* on ABC television one night, I was drawn into an eerie world of loss and memory; a world familiar and yet strange. A world vanished, but not gone. I thought again of Carl Jung and how he saw enduring power in energy: 'energy never vanishes ... [it] does not cease to exist when it disappears from consciousness'.

In 2016, Indigenous artist Jonathan Jones recreated a part of Australia lost, and reclaimed it as sacred space. He reimagined this world back into being. He reinterpreted the past as he reassembled it and he gave us a new way of seeing the possibilities of reconciliation. He called it *barrangal dyara* (*skin and bones*), a vast work of sculpture that stretched across 20,000 square metres of the Royal Botanic Garden in Sydney. This has been described as a work of 'immense loss', a lament for the destruction of culture. But it was more than that; it was a work of healing and survival.

This was a synthesis of white and black, and it spoke to the futility of trying to dominate a place when our presence can so easily be erased. This wasn't simply Indigenous space, Jones opened a tear in our universe that would allow us all to find new meaning in what it is to belong.

Palace of Memories followed Jones as he exhumed what was once a nineteenth-century palace on the shore of Sydney Harbour. I had no idea it had even existed. It seemed so incongruous; just a century earlier this was a place undisturbed. But in the early 1880s this palace dominated all around it. Nature yielded to this new enormous man-made presence. It grew out of a need of a people, just a few generations old on this land, to claim ownership; to boast of conquest. Henry Parkes, who would become the Father of Federation, commissioned it. The 'Garden Palace' would announce this new nation to the world.

I went in search of this place and found a newspaper article, 'The Most Beautiful Building You've Never Heard Of'. It was modelled on London's Crystal Palace and was built in 1879 for the Sydney International Exhibition. It was designed by colonial architect, James Barnet, and was said to be the length of two football fields. Searching out images of it, I was stunned. It was breathtaking, redolent of the great buildings of Europe. The *Sydney Morning Herald* at the time said it reminded one 'of the fabled palace of Aladdin in the *Arabian Nights*'. At its centre was a dome, 65 metres high. Two thousand men had worked day and night over eight months to complete it.

The exhibition was a showcase of this country to the world. It celebrated Australia's burgeoning exports of wool, wheat and gold. There were pieces of machinery and the finest porcelain. The exhibition opened to a song specially composed for the occasion, with the refrain, 'How Like England We Can Be?' But this exhibition also connected people to a much older history. It displayed the artefacts of the First People, so many of whom by now had been scattered from the shores of Sydney. There were weapons and shields: a reminder that people had lived here, had traded and fought here well before Europeans arrived.

Then, just three years later, at dawn on a September day in 1882, it burned to the ground. Flames roared so high into the sky and the heat was so intense that windows cracked in nearby streets. Thousands of people lined the streets to stand and watch. The *Evening News* reported: 'Many were lamenting and regretting the inevitable destruction of what had given so much pleasure to them, and had carried the name and doings of the people of this country into the Empires and most distant countries.'

White and black Australians were joined in this destruction. Everything can be lost, so easily. The fire was a reminder that nothing lasts and all can be taken away. But what is left? Jonathan Jones used thousands of bleached white shields to symbolise the rubble of the palace and the bones of Aboriginal people who had perished – been destroyed – that this nation could be born. Jones reconstructed the site using the shields to mark the boundaries, covering the spaces with coarse Kangaroo grass that grows in dense tufts, and he filled the silence with Indigenous languages presumed to be lost. Jones asked the question: If a nation can so easily erase such a building from its memory, what else can it forget? He explored how we live with absence and how it informs us anyway. The absent really isn't absent at all. The artist drew on the power of land and our place in it – all of us. This was history – ours, black and white – now given new meaning: an Australian story; a story of how the past is always with us and how we live with our loss.

Jonathan Jones says the 'rise and demise of the Garden Palace was part of the whole nation's identity at the time', and that by recreating the Palace he was providing 'a highway to nationhood'. He was reminding us that possession is fleeting and that place is all that remains. Jones provided a window into the missing piece of our national narrative. It wasn't a story of politics, it was deeper than that. What was it the Scottish politician and writer Andrew Fletcher said? 'If I could write all the songs, I would not care who wrote the laws.' Jonathan Jones doesn't seem to care for politics, his is a song for a country.

He is a gentle soul, Jonathan. Like me he draws his heritage from the Wiradjuri and Kamilaroi peoples. But, like me, he is also from the other side of the frontier. Like me, he is as white as he is black. I am sure that to look at him, most people would be oblivious to his heritage. He is not someone we would see as recognisably black. But what is that anyway? White, black: they are words, categories, that cannot possibly hold us.

Jonathan has grown close to my father; he has learned the Wiradjuri language from Dad. My father helped revive the language of his forebears, a language that was fast being lost. I remember something he said once: language doesn't tell you who you are, but where you are. Language is place. That is Jonathan's journey, to breathe in this place, to speak it and return it to us all. Indigenous people have many leaders who seek meaningful political change, but the artist reminds us that first we need also a story that binds us all to this land.

Australian writers, film-makers and artists have long grappled with this sense of place. The European presence here is fundamentally haunted by the act of invasion and dispossession. It is unsettled by the myth of terra nullius, a legal fiction (later overturned by the High Court *Mabo* ruling) that this was an empty land free for the taking.

Australian scholar David Tacey sees our nation as immature, inauthentic, although 'the land itself is ancient and powerful'. 'This spirit of place,' he writes, 'is not mystical, it is social and geo-political.' He points to the film *Picnic at Hanging Rock* – a story of vanishing into land – as creating a 'grinding tension between the colonial overlay of society and the unconscious substratum of ancient and denied realities'.

Picnic at Hanging Rock and *Palace of Memories* are each a meditation on what scholars Ken Gelder and Jane Jacobs have dubbed 'Uncanny Australia'. In the book of the same name, published in the late 1990s, they posed questions about how 'Aboriginal sacredness manifests itself in the public domain of the modern nation'.

They saw Australia as 'unsettled', disturbed by the recognition of the 'Aboriginal sacred'. The acknowledgment of native title after the *Mabo* decision raised questions about 'who is marginal – who is empowered enough to claim to represent the nation, and who feels as if the nation has disdained them'.

Gelder and Jacobs noted the unease of pastoralists and miners who, in a reversal of fortune, suddenly felt themselves dispossessed and embattled. Even the majorities, they wrote, could 'feel that they are precariously placed'.

'Home' was turned upside down, into 'something else, something less familiar and less settled'. This is the essence of the uncanny, a concept drawn from Freud, meaning 'to be at the same time in place and out of place'.

This is what Jonathan Jones sought to capture in his art. A building once designed to showcase Australia to the world, to capture within it Indigenous objects and thus Indigenous people, burned to the ground and forgotten, and into this space the possibility of imagining ourselves again – of rethinking our spirit of place. Jones was inviting us all to ponder how our stories connect, the ancient and the new.

In the documentary we are told Jones is an artist who refuses categorisation. Yes, Indigenous, but also through his work questioning and redefining what that is and inviting all people on this land to imagine a deep sense of belonging.

This doesn't mean we all become Indigenous or that we become more homogeneous but we can dwell in this 'uncanny'. We can as psychoanalyst Julia Kristeva says discover our 'incoherences and abysses' to come to terms with the 'stranger in ourselves'.

The stranger in ourselves.

That's what I was coming to terms with at Lake Mungo; it is what has drawn me to the work of Jonathan Jones: not my

Aboriginal ancestry or my European heritage, something else, something more elusive that can't easily be measured in DNA. It is that part of me where black and white meet and how what has happened here between us, has happened on this land. This is our home: unsettled and uncanny.

THE STORY OF US

I was about fifteen when I saw the film *Picnic at Hanging Rock*. My aunt – my dad's sister – took me to the cinema in Griffith. I could probably have counted on one hand how many times I had been to a movie; there was never any money spare for luxuries like this. I don't know why she took me and I don't know why to this film. But it was a rare treat, Jaffas and all. Beyond that was the film itself, and how it reached inside me and left me pondering questions that I have spent a lifetime trying to answer.

It was the music that grabbed me first, those pan pipes eerily floating over that parched Australian landscape. The film seeped into my consciousness. It was as much a dream as a film; it unnerved me. I didn't make the connection at the time – not intellectually at least – but I was left feeling as if the world itself had turned. This was about who we are as Australians; who we are in a place that is profoundly unsettled.

I can see now what I could not see then: this is a dreaming story – not white, not black – it is a dreaming for an Australia still becoming. This is a story of initiation: a profound rite of passage. It is a haunting meditation on place, with the vanishing girls seemingly swallowed by the land itself. Remember the voice-over of one of the doomed girls: 'What we see and what we seem are but a dream ... a dream within a dream.'

The girls, when they disappeared, became part of the rock itself. There is something deeply Hegelian about it all. How strange that the dreaming in an ancient land could connect with a nineteenth-century German philosopher. But Georg Wilhelm Friedrich Hegel spoke of becoming: he spoke of man 'not being at home in the world'. *Picnic at Hanging Rock* has always struck me as a film about what Hegel would have seen as our inevitable process of change. Hegel believed in a three-stage process, what he called a dialectic, in which we move from thesis to antithesis to synthesis: an unceasing quest for freedom and recognition. This, he believed, was the engine of history; a quest for an absolute spirit. And that's how I see *Picnic at Hanging Rock*: the thesis of Britishness set against the antithesis of terra nullius – an empty land for the taking. Those who emerge from the disappearance of the girls are forever changed: the synthesis of a new people in a new place.

Peter Weir's film, perhaps even more than Joan Lindsay's novel, revealed the incongruity of imposed Britishness on a harsh, hot, foreboding place: Europeans trying to tame an untameable country. Weir's camera focuses on an army of ants, or dwells on the light peering through the branches of a tree. He allows the wind and birdsong to punctuate the silence. In this way he grapples with the themes of alienation and belonging.

The Indigenous presence is felt more than seen: the land itself represented as blackness.

This is what shook me at Lake Mungo, that ancient place of old bones; it is what haunts me when I go back home and stand by the Murrumbidgee River, gazing at the stars. It is emptiness and being all at once. It is terra nullius and my deep need to fill the unfilled space. This is Freud's uncanny: when home suddenly becomes very strange.

It is a strangeness that lies out of the reach of science. I like to think that I am a man of reason; I prefer to put my faith in what I can test and see, what I can measure. But there are things beyond our grasp. Science can tell us what is, but it can't tell us what we feel. As Freud spoke of the uncanny, his one-time friend and later rival, Carl Jung, looked to the metaphysical. To Jung we had become cut off from nature. In turn we have become cut off from each other.

In film and literature and poetry and art we reach for those deeper connections. We want to know we are not alone. But the things we do to each other on this earth keep us that far apart. Story: it is the essence of being.

The British-Indian writer Salman Rushdie once said of the importance of stories: 'Those who do not have the power over the story that dominates their lives, the power to retell it, rethink it, deconstruct it, joke about it, and change it as times change, truly are powerless because they cannot think new thoughts.'

As our world spins around us, consumed as we are by political upheaval, economic uncertainty, terrorism and war, I have wondered about this thing: story and its importance. What is this great story of us? What captures this thing of life? This transcendence; this beauty and terror; this hope and despair; this fleeting performance measured in minutes before the curtain falls and we fade into the black and others mount the stage.

In a world
full of
temporary things you are
a perpetual feeling

The Indian poet Sanober Khan speaks of our need to find solace in nostalgia; to create the everlasting from fleeting moments. She says, 'the magic fades too fast ... but nothing remains ... nothing lasts.'

I contemplate that now as I think of us: people from all points tossed together here on this island to become a people, a country: a nation. Nothing remains ... nothing lasts. Yet, despite this impermanence, we struggle as human beings to make sense of ourselves and our place on this earth. When all passes, all too soon, what is left is the fact of our humanity and how we embraced it; the time we had and how it was spent. Each age asks much of us: we have been tested by war, and horror unimaginable except that our imaginations are what gave rise to it; we have endured disaster, collapse, tyranny, poverty, and above it all we endure. As Sanober Khan tells us, we 'create the everlasting from fleeting moments'.

The greatest story of us? For me it isn't written or spoken; for me it is a painting on a ceiling in a world far from my own. My epiphany came in the Sistine Chapel. There, in a throng of tourists crammed into the Vatican, I gazed at our eternal struggle. Michelangelo laboured four years to produce this, his depiction of Genesis. Here is the outstretched hand of Adam, reaching for the hand of God. They extend but they do not touch. Between them is all of us: all we want to be; all we fail to be; all our ambiguity. Between them is the very spark of life – not in the fact of existence but the act of striving.

It is twenty years since I gazed on Michelangelo's masterpiece, and I have never ceased pondering that distance – what is it that separates us, even as we reach for each other? To me it has always seemed that we live in that small, empty space, reaching for that connection, between the certainty of ourselves and the possibilities of togetherness. How do we fill that space? We fill it with history, identity, hate, myth, longing, love, resentment, memory. We reach for each other and yet we don't touch. Hegel would see it as the struggle for our freedom – that space, the essence of our being and non-being.

I glimpse that in Michelangelo's Adam and God – a vision of endless possibility. World history, wrote Hegel, is the 'interpretation of spirit in time'. The Nobel Prize-winning Polish poet Czeslaw Milosz wondered about this journey of time and people, this quest of the spirit. In his poem 'The Spirit of History', from A Treatise of Poetry, he writes:

> Amid thunder, the golden house of *is*
> Collapses, and the word *becoming* ascends.

He sees a world beyond certainty, and ahead, possibility and change: inevitable, unrelenting change. As Milosz writes:

> You without beginning, you always between …

Always between … that is me. For much of my life I saw that as an uncomfortable place to be; a place without rest. Without certainty. But I have no need of certainty now. In that space of becoming and between is a world of possibility. It is a world where I can write my story free of the constraints that others may put upon me. I can live here with the unresolved, the irreconcilable. The world need not make sense, any more sense than the crazy mix of DNA that makes me who I am. This is me, all of it; all of that contradiction mocks the idea of permanent, essential, unchanging identity.

I have come to be suspicious of that word, identity. It is true that we all seek identity: which communities we belong to; which football club we follow; what music we like; how we dress; where we live; religion; race; culture. All of this gives us a sense of who we are, somewhere to belong. But there is a darker side to identity, a stifling conformity; an us and them; identity that pits us against each other. It keeps returning me to that question: am I Australian? Am I Aboriginal? Can those things be the same?

I am an Australian – yet my history tells me that my sense of citizenship and belonging is fragile and fraught. I belong to a nation; I belong to family and a people and yet I am an individual free to determine for myself who and what I wish to be. Kwame Anthony Appiah is a Ghanaian-British philosopher who has spent a lifetime exploring the vexed questions of identity. Like me he has walked the line between race and history, in much of his writing I hear my own thoughts. He once wrote 'the shaping of my life is up to me'.

But how do I do that? I am an individual – I value that fiercely. John Stuart Mill said the value of the individual is the cornerstone of liberty – only people who are free can fully command their lives. As Mill once wrote, 'He who chooses his plan for himself, employs all his faculties.' Yet the freedom to choose was taken from me when Australia had already settled on what I was: black, a half-caste, an outcast; I was not born into Australia. My identity was already determined and I have spent a lifetime working my way free.

Appiah says identities make ethical claims – we live our lives as gay or straight or male or female, black or white (sometimes those categories themselves are blurred) – less certain. Appiah asks, do identities curb our autonomy or provide its contours? To be Aboriginal must I reject Australia? To be Australian must I put aside history? Must I forget? History and justice, these are ideas that in the past years I have returned to again and again.

This is not my story alone, it is the story of Australia. It is what our great storytellers have wrestled with; how can we belong in a place so foreign, so strange? When a nation is founded in a great injustice – and a great injustice it remains, taking someone else's country – how do we find rest? How do we find peace? The Australian novelist Eleanor Dark captures that impermanence in her great trilogy 'The Timeless Land'. She explores the birth pains of modern Australia, and the upheaval for the First Peoples. She begins by imagining the moment of the coming of the whites. The boy Bennilong [sic] has come to the shore with his father. Only six years old, he is expected to act as a man.

> He was conscious of the world, and conscious of himself as
> a part of it, fitting into it, belonging to it, drawing strength
> and joy and existence from it, like a bee in the frothing
> yellow opulence of the wattle.

Dark imagines a blue cloudless sky, the sea a 'silver line', the surf breaking on the rocks. Bennilong was tired but his father did not notice; he kept his eyes peeled for the 'boat with wings'. He had been looking year after year, after that strange morning when a 'magic boat had flown into their harbour'. It had 'folded its wings like a seagull' and come to rest. From the boat came 'mysterious beings with faces pale as bones'. Bennilong had been told this story in corroboree: how these strangers came, and left just as suddenly.

It was long ago and for most people the memory of the 'magic boat' had faded, but Bennilong's father kept the story alive in his son, and so they came to stand on the rock and watch and wait for the white faces' eventual return. So vivid is Dark's recreation that I feel as though I am the young boy himself, standing with his father, his head filled with old stories and imagining, dreaming and becoming.

> Bennilong stared at it. The unending water. He looked up at his father's lean figure, still motionless, still watching for the boat with wings, and there was born in him a conviction which all through his boyhood was to tease him now and then – that the water was not really unending after all; that somewhere, far, far away there lay another land; that someday he, Bennilong, not in a bark canoe but in a boat with wings, would go in search of it.

I don't think any writer has captured more eloquently or deeply the essence of becoming Australian than Eleanor Dark. I say *becoming* because that's what she imagined, not endings but something new – beginnings. She was a writer who embraced uncertainty. When I read her I don't read a white story or a black story but a story of place; it is a timeless land not a timeless people she seeks. Dark is telling us that if we are to call this place home, then we must make our peace with the land itself. Her trilogy deals with the birth of this new nation; how two peoples so different, separated by skin and language and culture – yet for all that intensely, recognisably human – meet and find each other. In her books, the First Peoples are alive, they lose the stilted quality, the remoteness and distance of so much historical writing.

Too often in our history Indigenous people are people being done unto, not doing. They are curiosities or a conundrum. Of course for much of our history, the story of what happened here was silenced. Aboriginal people melted from the frontier. Even in later histories that looked to revise our nation's story, Aboriginal people were depicted as victims, at the mercy of the brutality of settlers. But they were doing things, they were working and trading and having children, often with the newcomers. They were reading the Bible and they were surviving. Eleanor Dark captures the inner lives of two peoples – white and black – on the most remote corner of the world: this timeless land.

Land. It is land that holds them, that shapes them. The first book in the trilogy, also named *The Timeless Land*, traces the lives of Bennilong, his wife Barangaroo, the first governor, Arthur Phillip, and the runaway convict, Prentice. She pictures Phillip, lying awake at night, 'his light still burning by his bedside, his tired mind wrestling with a thousand cares'. He felt 'the utter strangeness of this land in which he found himself, and he remembered the name given to it by earlier explorers, and he said under his breath, looking at the gaunt still branches of a gum-tree outlined against the sky: "Terra Australis Incognita".' Dark's Phillip 'felt a power which was even stronger than the power of his race, an influence of the land itself – the strange land, the terra incognita.'

The entire book is a meditation on place. Each character struggles with their sense of self, when all certainty has been removed. For Prentice, this country represents a chance at freedom, to slip his chains and escape. He leaves the camp and strikes out for the distant mountains, that no one thought could be crossed. He is changed by the country. He meets an Aboriginal woman, together they have a child. It is not a loving relationship, he is too brutal and brutalised, but it is so human. Their child is a new type of Australian, something becoming: a synthesis. Prentice is gripped with fear by this place, the only home he will now ever know. Dark writes:

> It was as if this land, whose silence had always baffled
> him, had become articulate at last ... The land had taken
> him, used him, fashioned new life from him; his blood
> and his breath, were now, even when he died, a part of it
> forever.

As Phillip prepared to leave for England, his job here done, Dark depicts him as a ghost. England, his home, felt more than distant: it felt unreal. It was as if it had never existed. He no longer shared its stars or its seasons. This land, he said wearily, 'would settle in its own time'. Dark has Phillip pondering again the harshness of this country and the fate of those who would now never return to England:

> How long would it be, he asked himself wonderingly, before
> the people of his race could know it as their own? As aliens
> they had come to it, and as aliens they would die in it.
> Would it admit their children? Or their children's children?

Why am I so captivated by Eleanor Dark's *The Timeless Land*? For the same reason that Inga Clendinnen's metaphor of dancing on the beach speaks so powerfully to me. It is the possibility of the space between us. Many have written of the white experience or the black, as if that is all we are and all we will ever be, when in fact we were changing; changed by this land and by each other. I am reminded of something the Australian poet Robert Wood has said, that we *must find our own dead*. It is as if my voice can only be the voice of all of my ancestors.

A generation after Eleanor Dark, another Australian writer, Thomas Keneally, in his book *The Chant of Jimmie Blacksmith*, imagines a scene long after the whites have come. For Keneally's Jimmie Blacksmith, the golden house of *is* indeed has collapsed, and Blacksmith emerges as a new type of being, a creation possible only here. The bone-pale face of the white stranger has darkened, and the curly hair of Dark's Bennilong has straightened. This is the Australian synthesis: Blacksmith born of black and white – from ancient and new – Australian in a way that no other can be.

As Keneally writes, half-breed Jimmie had resulted from a visit some white man made to Brentwood blacks' camp in 1878.

Keneally's Blacksmith was based on a historical figure, Jimmy Governor. The real Jimmy was a mixed-race Wiradjuri man who, like his fictional equivalent, married a white woman and searched for a place in this new country, on the eve of Federation. Governor found instead derision and rejection, his wife endured humiliation, and Jimmy – aided by his brother and an uncle – responded with a violent rampage that ended with nine people dead and sparked the biggest manhunt in Australian history.

Keneally sees his Jimmie as the man between, finding a place in neither the white nor black world. He is a potent symbol of a country in transition; what has been and what is to come. In one scene Keneally depicts two office clerks debating Federation as Jimmie looks on, awaiting an instructional pamphlet on what wood to use for fencing. The clerks fall into a discussion about the American Civil War.

> 'It'd never happen here. Could yer imagine Australians shooting at Australians?'
> '… And you seem to forget, my friend, that there's no such thing as an Australian …'

They eventually notice Jimmie.

> 'Jacko?' he called. 'He's an honest poor bastard but he's nearly extinct.'
> 'And, surprisingly, that is the work of those you so fancifully call Australians.'

Keneally grapples with this emerging nation, a people in a process of 'becoming'. His Jimmie Blacksmith is as much a part of this transformation as the two arguing clerks. Rejected, he massacres the Australians who would tell him he was not one of them. However this nation was founded, whatever the injustice and brutality of British settlement, Jimmie is tied inexorably to its fate even as he is mocked, excluded and doomed. Even as he so violently rejects it.

In film and art and song and literature we have sought to make sense of what it is to be this thing called an Australian. Eleanor Dark, Tom Keneally and Peter Weir: they have tried to tell the story of us – of our place. They set us in an ancient continuum ruptured by a cataclysmic clash of culture and civilisation. Out of destruction we are born anew: uncertain perhaps of our place, but with no other place to call our own. Whiteness must struggle with its blackness; it is in the land itself, it is in the memory of the people displaced. And it is there in our blood: hidden blackness, or blackness denied.

Those of us who identify as Indigenous, as First Peoples, we too grapple with our whiteness. It is there in our skin; no longer black but lighter now. Sometimes, we are indistinguishable from any other white person. For us it is about fashioning or refashioning what it is to belong, when the very essence of belonging has been ruptured and the certainty of heritage blurred. Jimmy Governor (Jimmie Blacksmith) is part white, married white and yet is rejected for being black. What it is to be Indigenous has become a puzzle not easily explained, nor simple to comprehend. These are questions I am left to ponder as well.

The young Indigenous writer Ellen van Neerven, in her book of short stories, *Heat and Light* – a dazzling collection that crunches genre and gender, where plants speak as people and the past and future collide – grapples with ambiguity and the fluidity of identity and belonging. Van Neerven is of Aboriginal and Dutch heritage, and many of these stories are tales of living in-between.

'So much is in what we make of things,' she writes. 'The stories we construct about our place in our families are essential to our lives.' In the story of a girl looking for herself in the image of a grandmother she never knew, van Neerven writes, 'If I didn't know my grandmother, then how could I know myself?'

These storytellers I have been drawn to – these Australian storytellers – they are not Indigenous or non-Indigenous, they are not black or white; that's not how I see them. To me they are a connection, an unbroken tradition that begins when humans first speak and carve drawings on a cave wall. There are writers who cannot get past politics; who use words to settle scores. But politics favours certainty and we don't live our lives in straight lines. Politics needs an enemy, but for me at least, the 'enemy' lives in me.

Storytellers work with and against history. In history we find difference and conflict, yet the storyteller must find us in each other. As Robert Wood says, 'I is one of the most misleading words' in our language, it 'means you to so some degree because it is in Others that we see ourselves'. Wood is someone who could be identified as 'mixed race', his mother's family from Asia, but as he says he has 'passed as a white man for most of my life'. In his poetry he looks beyond the clichés of identity, 'there has always been a little bit of curry in Scotland, always a little bit of whiskey in Kerala … We are in one world still, even if we code switch at will.'

Wood, like myself, eschews certainty for ambiguity. It is that space – that elusive but luring in-between – the ship and the shore – that entices him as it entices me. Nothing stands still. 'Historically, Australia is a colony,' he writes, 'but the sands are shifting.' In those shifting sands we find loss, emptiness, place, home; we find each other.

The French historian Michel de Certeau says we live with a history of absence. We use stories to fill the void. What we call history he saw as a collection of artefacts we assemble to try to make sense of ourselves. Here is the crux of recognition, constructed out of a past reimagined, history written and history denied. As a nation, we struggle to reconcile ourselves to our past and our place. Always there is story.

The story of Australia speaks to us from the dry shores of Lake Mungo. Forty thousand years ago, the waters were full, sustaining a thriving community. Here a man was laid to rest with full ceremony, his body smeared in ochre. In all of humanity this was rare, among the earliest examples of such ritual. The mourners sang a song in language now lost.

As modern Australia celebrated its birth at Federation in 1901, the historical inspiration for Jimmie Blacksmith, the real Jimmy Governor, sat in a Darlinghurst jail cell, alternating between singing songs in his traditional Wiradjuri language and reading the Bible – the synthesis of the old and new worlds that collided here so violently, given form in a man soon for the gallows. It is a synthesis Keneally saw as contradiction; and yet it is the essence of being Australian.

Joan Lindsay wrote the book of the missing girls of Hanging Rock, and director Peter Weir fixed it in our imaginations. The land itself, a potent character in an ethereal tale of place and being.

These are Australian stories, ancient and modern, and all efforts at recognition – a need to be seen. It is indeed a fleeting project, an attempt to capture a people – a people always changing – in a time and place. A drawing on a cave wall preserved for antiquity, to tell future people: 'This was us.'

It is so human, and it is essential.

PART 2
FAMILY

FINDING FRANK FOSTER

I have written often about Frank Foster; his life has mesmerised me. I have wondered at the world he saw around him; how rapidly it changed and how his life was shaped by those changes. I have been trying to find Frank Foster for half my life. He has been the missing part of me. I have felt his presence like a phantom limb; an itch I cannot scratch. Frank Foster appears in my life so briefly and from a long time past, yet had he not existed I would not be who I am.

He is a connection to a time that is with us still, a time that defines us as a nation even as there are those who would reject it. That time we call settlement or invasion; which, we imagine, defines who we are. The past cannot be removed; it can't be wished away. We look back on it through the eyes of our age; we see a time and a place but we lose sight of the people. They become caricatures, figures onto whom we project ourselves. We see what we want to see, we choose sides; we are on the shore or the ship.

I think of Frank Foster as the first Australian in my family. Could there be a more English-sounding name: Frank Foster. I have no idea from whom he took the name; somewhere, at some point, there was a white man and a black woman and who they were – their DNA – lives in me. For certain, Frank's grandparents would have been among those who saw the tall ships; who looked for the first time on the faces of these pale strangers. I have scoured the lists of the early arrivals to colony; there is no Foster in either the First or Second Fleets. But then there it is among the convicts of the Third Fleet in 1791: Samuel Foster. Could that be the man, Frank's grandfather?

Until recently I knew so little of Frank Foster, this man who was my great-great-grandfather. Now Frank has spoken, as if he were standing next to me. I met a man whose family history wraps around mine and has opened a window onto a past that illuminates so much of our present.

Frank Foster emerges from the Australian frontier. He was a boy among the huddled remnants of the blacks of Sydney. Born not one hundred years since the coming of the whites. He existed on rations and wrapped himself in blankets handed out to his people, believed doomed for extinction.

Frank and his family took shelter around Circular Quay. He lived with his father, also named Frank, and his mother Elizabeth Matto, an Aboriginal woman, and two sisters, Bella and Bessie. The blacks had taken up makeshift camps all over the Sydney shoreline, clinging to old tracks and places as a city took shape around them.

He was ten years old when his father died and the world he knew fell. Old Frank had been visiting a nearby Aboriginal camp and his death was recorded in the Sydney *Daily Telegraph* of 29 April 1880. Reading the report today gives me a glimpse into a New South Wales colony in transition; a Sydney where the black past was not yet pushed from sight but rubbed embarrassingly against a people who were already taking on airs and graces.

For some weeks past a camp has been formed at Double Bay
by a few of the aborigines who are wandering about Sydney.
Yesterday one of the men inhabiting the camp, a half-caste
named Frank Foster, died and as no doctor had attended
him an inquest will be held upon the remains today. The
death was reported to the police, by whom the body was
removed to the dead house, awaiting the inquest.

Fatherless, Frank, his sisters and their mother were rounded up
and sent far away to a new Aboriginal mission at Maloga on the
Murray River. Here they would be hidden away, the pillow
smoothed for their demise. For those who survived, here they
would be 'Christianised' and 'civilised'. On the mission Frank
was told if he had a future at all it would be as one of the so-
called 'Half Castes'; those whose drop of white blood might open
the door to their eventual disappearance into a world where all
trace of the black past would be lost. Frank and his sisters were
schooled by the missionaries. The records show he was a diligent
and bright boy. He had ambitions to be a teacher himself.

I can track Frank's footprints through the official records of
the day. By 1889 he had moved to the New South Wales south
coast; the Aboriginal people of the coast were entwined with
those of the Sydney region. His family links would have reached
into these lands. He joined two people, Hugh and Ellen
Anderson, who had established a bark hut school for Aboriginal
kids in Kangaroo Valley. Here he realised his dream of being a
teacher. Again, I find him in the government records. An
education official was sent to observe one of Frank's classes. His
report describes Frank Foster as 'an intelligent half-caste'. It says
he reads and spells well and conducted a class in subtraction.

Frank moved through the missions crisscrossing New South Wales and Victoria. The names – Cummeragunja, Warangesda – a shadow world where my people didn't die out but regrouped and formed new families that live on today. At each stop Frank sought to teach. At Warangesda he met an Aboriginal girl named Lydia Naden and they had a daughter, Florence. I remember Florence as an old lady living on the Three Ways mission in Griffith. We called her 'Nanny Cot', she was my father's grandmother. We would visit her each weekend. Her mind was slipping, the memories growing dim, but she would smile and touch our hands, connecting me to a timeless sense of belonging.

Florence lived her life without her father. Frank was banished from Warangesda for being impudent and refusing to obey the mission managers. They would not allow him to teach and saw his demands for his people's rights as an unwelcome disruption. From Warangesda Frank Foster's tracks leave our family. I had known of him – just a name. The schoolteacher, my family called him. But there was nothing to give flesh to this name. At each turn the trace of him grew more faint. Until I unlocked a secret history I had always yearned for.

I was training at the gym at Redfern's National Centre of Indigenous Excellence. I go there not just for fitness but to be with other Aboriginal people, to be renewed by a sense of community. I began talking to a young man, Alan Daly, who I would often see. Usually we would nod and move on, but this day we stopped and over half an hour mapped our families. This is how we meet; Aboriginal people tracing our songlines, establishing our boundaries and confirming our identities.

Alan is from La Perouse in Sydney, and I am from western New South Wales, but I told him of an old connection, of a man named Frank Foster. Alan smiled and said, 'I know him, I have something for you.'

Later that day he sent me a timeline, part of a community project to breathe life into people long gone, to sing the songs of old ancestors. Here were the missing chapters of Frank's story. It told of how he wandered after Warangesda, moving from one community to another. He married several times and had more children; like so many other black men he found himself in jail, and he spent his last years as a fisherman on the south coast.

He lived at the Aboriginal mission at Roseby Park and died in 1941. He is buried in the graveyard in the town of Berry. The funeral notice describes him as a 'well known and respected identity … and a great sufferer'.

What a life he had led, what things he had seen. A boy of the brutal frontier who carried his swag through missions and dreamed of his books and his teaching. He was born into his people, robbed of their land. He saw a new country – Australia – born and looked to find a place among it. He lost his home and searched for a new one. He loved and lost children.

But he leaves me a deep legacy. The Fosters are a large Aboriginal family, extending from La Perouse to the New South Wales south coast. I am proud to count myself among them. But there are many thousands of Fosters throughout Australia. Somewhere there is a branch of this family tree – white Fosters – that shares a bloodline with me. Somewhere our paths separated. Black was black and white was white, and Frank Foster was somewhere between: a black man with a white man's name.

How foolish to talk of identity that divides us. We cannot say that you are that and I am this. Our history, our blood, mocks us. There are so many others on all sides of my family, black and white. Who am I supposed to embrace, who do I deny? How far back do we go? At some point, geneticists tell us we all came from one place, a place in Africa. We moved across the globe, weaving in and out of each other's stories for tens of thousands of years, and that endless journey brought us here to this island and this is our home and we are a people.

THE EVERYWHEN

The ancient Greek thinker Heraclitus is said to have led a lonely life. He is typically depicted as 'the weeping philosopher', hands tightly clasped as he pondered the eternal question of change: what moves our universe? He is considered one of the founders of ontology, the study of being. What is it to exist? How do we account for our differences? Heraclitus is famous for his saying, 'No man ever steps in the same river twice'. In that sentence he asks us what it is to be human; it is not enough that we simply be, we are in an endless process of becoming. Heraclitus poses questions not just of the man crossing the river, but the river itself. Is what we call the river defined by the body of water? At that moment that we step from the bank, is that the river? When that water rushes by, when someone downstream also wades in, is that then the same river? We exist in a time and a place and then it is gone. A river is not simply a river, a man is not just a man; nothing is permanent, nothing is fixed.

The German philosopher Hegel applied Heraclitus's lesson to the movement of history. We are forever changing, driven by a quest for freedom and recognition. Thesis turns to antithesis and then to synthesis. I have written earlier of Czeslaw Milosz, he was as much philosopher as poet steeped in ideas of *becoming* more than *being*. That is not a subtle distinction; *being* implies something fixed or permanent, *becoming* is always changing, out of catastrophe we endure. We find new life beyond the crumbling 'golden house of *is*'.

This was the world that confronted my ancestors in the nineteenth century. Theirs was indeed a world of becoming. Violence and disease had wrought havoc. My great-great-grandfather Frank Foster had been moved from mission to mission, far from the land of his birth, longing for a life of learning always just out of his reach. It wasn't just my black ancestors who were living through tumultuous change. John Grant, a seventeen-year-old rebel from Tipperary, Ireland, was banished to the colonies for life. He came in chains, his other family members executed for murder and rebellion, and would never again see his country. This was his home now. He fathered many children, had two wives, and died one of the largest landholders in New South Wales. It was said he was the wealthiest Irish Catholic in the colonies.

John Grant lived on the land of the Wiradjuri people, west of the Blue Mountains. Here the two sides of my family come together, in the wake of a battle that lasted several years, called at the time 'the Bathurst Wars' – as the *Sydney Gazette* described it, 'an exterminating war'. Much of the Wiradjuri population had been wiped out. When the colonial authorities handed out blankets to the survivors, among them were those with the name Grant. Within a generation, what we call Aboriginal society had been transformed. My ancestors told new stories of life in a world somewhere between black and white.

The colonial government did not know what to do with them. In the early 1880s a special body was formed, the Aborigines

Protection Board, with the intention of controlling the lives of all Aboriginal people in New South Wales. It tallied the Aboriginal population in the state at 8919 and divided it into classifications of 'Full-Blood' and 'Half-Caste'. The board's report of 1883 makes it clear that the 'Half-Castes', if they were to have a future, would be integrated (albeit at a menial level) into the state's economy. The Protector, George Thornton, said:

> I maintain the opinion I have always held with regard to the half-caste portion of the aborigines viz, that they should be compelled to work in aid of their own requirements. They are well able to do so, having strength, experience and intelligence to qualify them for it; whilst I am of the opinion that the pure black should be taught, encouraged and aided in doing something for his own sustenance and comfort.

Thornton was frustrated, describing the 'Half-Castes' as 'indolent' and 'useless'. He wanted them put to work to fill the colony's labour shortage. He called for the establishment of reserves, in effect migrant worker training camps, to enable them to 'form homesteads, to cultivate grain, vegetables, fruit'. Aborigines would become farmers. On 16 May 1892 the board received an application from 'William Grant, an Aboriginal' for a plot of land near Cowra. They called him Bill; on the missions in the area, he was known as the 'storyteller'. There are some old enough today to remember him and they tell me how he would keep people awake for hours around the campfire, telling stories of old times that had been handed down to him. I am told he would carry with him the stump of a ceremonial carved tree, an old artefact rescued as the land was cleared to make way for new farms. On Bill Grant's marriage certificate are listed Father: John Grant, squatter – the old Irishman; mother: an unnamed Aboriginal woman who marked the page with an 'x'. Bill Grant was my paternal great-grandfather.

Change is not always ours for the choosing. Our fate is tied to the elements, to fortune, to timing and the sweep of history. The archaeological records tell us that at least 65,000 years ago, people first stepped onto this continent. They are credited with having made the first open sea journey in the history of humanity. It is a trek that leads to me today. The historians of the Irish Grant family trace their lineage back at least a thousand years, to the ninth century in Florence. The Gherardini family were one of the founding clans of the Republic of Florence. The famous 'Mona Lisa' is said to be a portrait of Lisa Gherardini. The Gherardinis were believed to be one of the most ancient and wealthy families of the area; they were indigenous to Italy, either Etruscan or Roman. One historian described the Gherardinis of Montagliari (as they were known) as 'instigators of disorder'.

Otho Gherardini had been a Duke and a mercenary soldier who, according to legend, followed the caravan of King Canute of England as he passed through Florence after an audience with the Pope in Rome. Otho remained in Normandy, before eventually embarking for England with Edward the Confessor when he was called back from exile to become King of England. Otho Gherardini had a son he named Walter FitzOther; eventually that became Fitzgerald. The family story has it that some other branches of the family tree took the name Le Grand, then Le Grant until simply Grant. By the mid-eleventh century, the Grants and Fitzgeralds arrived in Ireland, the Grant family becoming the Barons of Iverk in Kilkenny. Centuries later they would be dispossessed by Oliver Cromwell's conquest of Ireland. The late Monsignor Leo Grant, a Catholic priest in Bathurst who curated the family tree, told me that after Cromwell 'the Grants became flotsam on the sea of Irish history, every generation being forced to move on by famine or civil unrest'.

I remember the first time I touched the ground of Ireland. I had been sent there as a reporter to cover the annual marching season, where Protestant and Catholic would confront each other, often violently. Each was playing their part in what the Irish called 'The Troubles' a sectarian blood feud that stretched back centuries and so altered my family's history. I had long been captivated by the Irish struggle, seeing in the Catholics – the blacks of Europe as they were known – a mirror of the Aboriginal fight for justice in Australia. I had read the story of Wolfe Tone, a seventeenth-century revolutionary figure who founded the Society of United Irishmen, the organisation my great-great-great-grandfather, John Grant, and his brother Jeremiah fought for. Tone was in fact a Protestant but he formed what he called a 'brotherhood of affection' for Catholics to throw open the doors of the Irish parliament. He took exile, and from France convinced the French government to seek to liberate Ireland. In 1796, he accompanied a flotilla of thirty-five French ships, carrying 12,000 men. They reached the Irish coast but the wind turned against them, they were battered by rain and snow and the fleet was broken up. Eventually the invasion was aborted. The Irish historian Thomas Pakenham quipped: 'It was a Protestant wind'.

When I landed in Ireland, I looked for something more, something deeper, a connection to my family's past. I stood in the streets of Belfast and willed myself to feel that I belonged. Does our DNA carry a genetic memory? Does home never really leave us, no matter how much time has elapsed? I think of those people I have met who discover a long-lost Aboriginal ancestor and construct an entirely new identity for themselves. It is what is called a Freudian history, a history of absence, a desire to find that missing part of ourselves: it is history as healing. Are they Aboriginal? If that's what they believe then it is their choice. Was I Irish? Of course not. But it mattered to me. It helped me write a page in a family story, whose chapters remain unwritten.

We are all of us a part of each other. We step into many rivers and are inevitably changed: a process of becoming. A Chinese friend once said to me that we are the last stop on our ancestors' journey. What does that make me? I have been a nobleman in old Florence; part of the Norman conquest of England; an Irish baron and then a cast-out peasant farmer. I have been a Catholic rebel, striking back at the harsh hand of Protestant England. I have been a Wiradjuri warrior defending an invasion by strangers with muskets. Yet I would be today unrecognisable to my forebears; someone who doesn't speak their languages or practise their ceremonies. I am a pinwheel of colours spinning into one; a kaleidoscope of history that came to rest on the shores of Botany Bay.

What a chain of events Otho Gherardini started when he set out from Florence. His descendants would sit with kings and eventually be clapped in chains and sent in a convict ship to a penal colony in New South Wales, on a continent where people had lived for tens of thousands of years. A branch of the Fitzgerald family would find themselves in America and marry into a family named Kennedy. John Fitzgerald Kennedy would sit in the White House as the thirty-fifth president of the United States. The Gherardinis are still a prominent family in Florence, and an Italian newspaper has written of the links between the Gherardini and Kennedy families. Myth, legend, secrets, names lost and changed, how much is truth? Such is the mystery of any family. What is undeniable is that none of us is from one place; our families' arteries are infused with the blood of countless and varied ancestors. The golden house of *is* collapses, and the word *becoming* ascends.

*

Why do we imagine that Indigenous people are somehow static, unchanging? Why does the arrival of the British signify an end to something and not a new beginning? It is remarkable that a people who had lived and adapted to the harshest, driest land on earth for countless thousands of generations would be thought to perish at the mere touch of modernity. It is clear from my own family that in fewer than fifty years we were transformed. We had new names, we read the Bible and spoke English. We were fishermen and farmers. Yet, by the twentieth century, a new generation of scholars studying Indigenous communities fixed a narrative that we were hapless victims of European expansion. We were a relic, a lost world of 'noble savages': a people for whom there was no more dreaming.

W.E.H. Stanner, the Australian anthropologist, was a remarkable man and writer who studied Aboriginal society up close and despaired at what he saw as its destruction. Stanner, in the 1960s, wondered where this ancient culture would sit in a world marked more by the trade of currency than ancient ceremony. Stanner believed that Aboriginal culture sat uncomfortably with Western notions of economy:

... The Dreaming and The Market are mutually exclusive.
What is the Market? In its most general sense it is a variable
locus in space and time at which values – the values of
anything – are redetermined as human needs make
themselves felt from time to time. The Dreaming is a set of
doctrines about values – the value of everything – which
were determined once and for all in the past.

Stanner conceived of the Dreaming as 'an heroic time of the
indefinitely remote past'. He coined the analogism
'everywhen' – something so old as to be timeless. He wrote, it
'has for them an unchallengeable sacred authority'. Determined
once and for all? Unchallengeable authority? How is this any
different from the stifling papal doctrine of fifteenth-century
Europe that led eventually to the Reformation, the Thirty Years
War and the creation of a new political order? How is
Indigenous society somehow immune from the great
philosophical revolution of the Enlightenment, which rejected
superstition for reason and science? Were Aboriginal people
forever fixed in this 'everywhen', condemned to perish as the
world turned around them?

Stanner explores this clash of cultures – dreaming and
market – in his captivating essay 'Durmugam: A Nangiomeri'. It
traces Stanner's encounters with a man – Durmugam – from
Daly River in the Northern Territory. The anthropologist meets
him 'one wintry afternoon in 1932'. Durmugam is painted with
earth pigment and brandishing weapons for a large-scale fight.
'The struggle could be seen to resolve itself into discontinuous
phases of duels ... my eyes were drawn and held by an
Aboriginal of striking physique and superb carriage.' The

Europeans called Durmugam 'Smiler,' an ironic nickname for a man widely feared and believed to be 'the most murderous black in the region'.

Stanner's essay spans the course of Durmugam's life and laments the decline of both the once-proud warrior and the traditions and beliefs that nurtured and sustained him. 'The High Culture had not prospered; many of the young men openly derided the secret life.' What Stanner observed was the transformation and decay that had begun after penetration of the region by foreigners in the 1870s. Aboriginal people had become 'more familiar with Europeans and more dependent on their goods'. He describes how the people began to 'wander elsewhere to look for new goods and excitement'. They developed a taste for European goods: tobacco, sugar, tea. Stanner describes their fascination with houses, vehicles and firearms.

The Nangiomeri were a people in transition, their numbers depleted, ravaged by disease, frontier violence and grog. Stanner describes survivors regrouping, separate clans forming new affiliations, old borders dissolving: 'some of the small tribes … had ceased to exist'. Stanner describes them as migrants, like migrants everywhere propelled by upheaval into an uncertain future. Durmugam worked in mining, construction, and cutting sleepers for the new rail lines. He clung to his traditions even as he blended into this new economy.

To Stanner this was devastating. 'The Aborigines were in chains,' he wrote, 'they could not bear to be without the narcotic tobacco and the stimulating tea; any woman could be bought for a fingernail of one or a spoonful of the other.' These people, he said, were 'as distant from the European as it was possible to be … inescapably connected to suffering'.

Through Stanner's eyes, Aboriginal people were not merely a people without a concept of 'time' or 'history' but an ahistorical people. They were indeed changeless. Stanner equated change with assimilation, assuming Aboriginal people would vanish, dissolved into European life. Stanner finally met Durmugam again as a 'white-haired' man of fifty-seven, with 'failing eyesight, but still erect and still a tall striking figure of a man'. The old warrior had lived in two worlds: his body was no longer painted with the earth, and the weapons of battle were laid down.

> The blacks were on wages and very money conscious; all had European clothes and in their camps … one could find gramophones, torches, kitchenware, even bicycles; some of the younger people, though unable to read, were fond of looking at comic papers and illustrated magazines.

Stanner failed to see synthesis or adaptation, he saw instead tradition crushed, 'culture was on its last legs'. No one personified this more than the once fearsome Durmugam; prestige gone, his family scattered, he was personally humiliated when his favourite wife ran off with the son of his first wife. He told Stanner he 'would be better off dead'.

Change, wherever it occurs, is often accompanied by tragedy. Think of the refugee setting out on a leaky boat, leaving behind her land and family, likely never to see them again. Think of the convict in chains, sent to a land he'd never heard of, with no prospect of return. This is the story of our world; there is not a people on our planet who have not at some time endured revolution, war, invasion or persecution. It is happening in our time, as we see the greatest forced movement of people since the end of World War Two. Yet we don't imagine them fixed in time. The Greek word *telos* speaks of an end or purpose, that history itself is progressive. Stanner saw a people without telos.

Stanner's essay has helped set Indigenous people in the Australian imagination: a people for whom change spells doom. It has all the hallmarks of the 'noble savage', the European ideal of a people unsullied by 'progress'. Stanner – for all his good intentions and empathy – robbed Aboriginal people of a future. His idea of people caught between the dreaming and the market exerted a powerful hold on policy makers as they sought to find the balance between economy and identity; between what is 'mainstream' and what is 'Indigenous'. It has helped shape ideas of identity, some Indigenous people embracing the idea of timelessness and rejecting of what is seen as modernity.

This has never been my story. My family and countless other Aboriginal families have navigated this new world, blending with it and forming part of the mosaic of a new Australia. Another anthropologist, Gaynor Macdonald, has studied my family's people, the Wiradjuri of New South Wales. She has rejected Stanner's assumptions. She says he underestimated the desire and ability of the Aboriginal people to change and develop because his own beliefs blinded him to their creativity and resilience. He saw only destruction and loss. Had he desired, he would have been able to see these transformations around him in many parts of Australia, including New South Wales in the 1950s. He was not looking for change. But because he did not see it, did not mean it was not happening.

FROM MISSIONS TO MIGRANTS

My paternal grandfather, Cecil Grant, was a man born in the first decade of the twentieth century onto the fringes of the frontier, a man whose life embodies the shift of Aboriginal people from outcasts on the edges of society, to take up a place in Australia. I have only faint memories of him; he died when I was only six years old. But he loomed large in my life; he was a tough man, a man of discipline and character. A man of deep Christian faith, and an enduring pride in being a Wiradjuri man – and those things were never in conflict.

He was at times a shearer, a rodeo bull rider, a rabbit trapper, a fruit picker and a soldier; his personal journey in a black migration from mission to town: a distance measured in miles but a trek measured in justice. He was a friend of Doug Nicholls, a famous footballer, then pastor, and later Sir Doug, Governor of South Australia. Doug Nicholls was a pivotal figure in the campaign for the 1967 referendum that had as its theme, 'Vote yes for Aborigines: they want to be Australians too.' My grandfather was also close to another seminal Aboriginal leader, Bill Ferguson, and together they campaigned for full citizenship for their people.

This was a time of great upheaval. The era of segregation was passing and now it was assumed Aboriginal people would be 'absorbed into the Commonwealth'. That was the phrase of the time, the thinking behind a policy of assimilation – something that is a dirty word now, akin to an ethnic cleansing, an attempt to make black people white. It is true that assimilation was often coercive, the fate of families determined by government officials, some given a 'pass' into white Australia, a home uptown, access to schools, while others remained in choking, oppressive missions. Children were removed from families with the intention of preparing them for the white world. There is a photograph that sticks in my mind. It is of three generations of one family, from a dark-skinned grandmother, to her lighter daughter, to her daughter's blond, blue-eyed son; an assimilationist's view of the Australian Dream.

Yet, there is another story here, a story of people who saw an open door and walked through; people like my grandfather. Listen to their voices. I can read about them in the magazine *Dawn*, published from the 1950s to the 1970s by the New South Wales Aborigines Welfare Board. I have no doubt they were carefully curated, yet they speak powerfully still. Most of them speak of their Christianity and economic empowerment. They call for fishing and economic cooperatives, for Aboriginal reserves to be turned into farms. As one wrote: 'If we can work farms for white men, we can do it for ourselves.'

They talk of their people needing to shoulder responsibility for their plight, and don't we hear that echoed today. All of the men stressed their work ethic, and their desire to find a place in modern Australia.

Another says: 'I've held numerous jobs from farmhand, fisherman, mill hand, factory worker, sewerage ganger, miner, to my present position and according to all reports, I am accepted everywhere.'

These are the powerful voices of Aboriginal economic migration. I have written about these people in a *Quarterly Essay* – 'The Australian Dream: Blood, History and Becoming'. I know these people, they are the people of my childhood who walked with a straight-backed dignity, and were unstinting in their demand for their rights. They didn't just demand equality. They assumed it. When I see them, I see individuals with choice, shaped by their world, as they in turn shaped the world around them. They were alive to the possibilities of life in an Australia whose economy was often booming.

They looked at the post-war migrant influx and hitched a ride, becoming economic migrants themselves. The meagre pay and menial work didn't dissuade them, as by their own admission they (often in desperation) fought to provide for their families. A dynamic and diverse Aboriginal population was emerging from these people in transition.

A decade ago the late academic Maria Lane probed this migration and the world it has created. She observed two diverging Indigenous populations. An Aboriginal woman, Lane was drawn to the emergence of a fledgling open society, as she called it. It was opportunity-, effort- and outcome-oriented, contrasting with what she called an embedded society, which was risk averse-, welfare- and security-oriented.

The two populations, she said, are linked through kinship and continuing interaction, but the course of their lives was set by the great Aboriginal economic migration. It was a slow grind but, she said, a new paradigm was surely emerging. These were the people on the move in the 1940s to the 1970s, leaving the settlements and throwing off the heavy hand of government control. Their journeys I've already traced through my family. The timing was crucial. Their movement coincided with periods of economic growth that increased their opportunity. As Lane said, it was a risky move into the unknown. But one that for most, paid off, just as it did for other economic migrants, drawn from the far-flung corners of the earth.

Lane picked up their story when the grandchildren and great-grandchildren of these pioneers were exploding into higher education. Focusing on South Australia, she found that in less than a decade, from the late 1990s to the mid-2000s, the number of Indigenous students entering the last year of high school doubled, and of those, the number gaining good university entrance scores had likely tripled. These kids, Lane says, were part of both white and black worlds, redefining what identity – indeed identities – meant for them.

At the same time, she pointed out, there was a parallel Aboriginal universe, an embedded shadow world of choking poverty, rivers of grog, frightening rates of violence, overcrowded housing and intergenerational unemployment. While the children of Lane's open society were graduating high school, their embedded society cousins were committing suicide at rates ten times higher than the rest of the Australian population. They were graduating, not from high school, but from juvenile detention to adult prisons.

In the embedded society were those who were left behind. Maria Lane mapped their journey too. Many had never left the settlements. Many had ventured into small towns and had then returned.

Many had simply missed the economic cycle and failed to grasp the full range of opportunities. Instead they became locked in cycles of welfare dependency and social decay. They became embedded.

There is great community and enduring bonds of family found in Lane's embedded society. I know these people. This is also my family. I know that they can be generous, loving and loyal, and life in the open society for us can be lonely, alienating. Even the most successful Indigenous peoples are not immune to random or hurtful racism.

Lane sometimes was guilty of ascribing too much of the fate of these two populations to the vagaries of personal choice, when in fact history, economy, timing and luck have often been far more decisive. Besides, no broad social sketch can be entirely accurate. Individuals are too unpredictable and there is a risk sometimes of caricature and stereotype. Yet she did identify a schism in our population, and it punctures the lazy and convenient assumption of a homogeneous Aboriginal society, where we are all the same. We are, in fact, like all other communities: lacerated by class, gender, geography. Our lives are shaped by fortune and resilience. Identity itself is never fixed.

Maria Lane left us a great gift, she breathed life into Aboriginal lives; dynamic, resourceful, courageous people striking out into a new world. This is the community I was raised in. Lane demolishes the idea that Indigenous people are forever trapped between *the Dreaming and the Market*. These pioneers were prepared to privilege *economy* over culture. They were open to change, they moved and they formed new communities as people the world over have done for millennia. They were *closing the gap*, before bureaucrats had ever coined the phrase, and inspired generations that came after them.

Between 1996 and 2006 the Indigenous community in Australia was transformed. Numbers of educated well-paid professionals exploded. In just a decade, they increased by nearly 75 per cent. That was more than double the increase in the non-Indigenous middle class. By 2006 more than 14,000 Aboriginal and Torres Strait Islanders between the ages of 20 and 64 were employed in professional occupations. That's 13 per cent of the total Indigenous workforce.

Dr Julie Lahn, from the Australian National University, looked at this phenomenon in her paper 'Aboriginal Professionals: Work, Class and Culture'. She said that Aboriginal professionals in urban centres remain largely overlooked. Dr Lahn saw this as a major shortcoming, impeding understanding of a transformation that is increasingly evident to Aboriginal people themselves. We see this in our universities. There are around 30,000 Indigenous university graduates in Australia. In 1991 there were fewer than 4000. That number is likely to double in the decade to come. We are now seeing a second generation of Indigenous PhDs. The emergence of this middle class, of which I am assuredly a part, presents new questions for identity.

That I am an Indigenous person is a fact of birth. That is who I am, but that is not all I am. The reality is more ambiguous, it defies easy definition, even as I may try to cloak it in a veil of certainty. To borrow from Franz Kafka, identity can be a cage in search of a bird. I was born into that 'half-caste' community that emerged from the Australian frontier; a hybrid society formed out of the clash of old and new. In that society they married each other, repopulated in the harsh segregated settlements designed to Christianise and civilise us.

In Mexico we would be known as *Mestizo*, or in Canada, *Métis* – people in-between, mixed. *Mestizo* comes from the Spanish word for miscegenation – the mixing of ancestries. In Mexico the *Mestizo* are an entirely new and distinct identity – not Spanish or wholly indigenous. The *Métis* trace their ancestry to the First Nations people and European settlers, usually French fur traders. The *Mestizo* have different and often greater legal status than indigenous people, reflecting the racial hierarchy of Spanish or Portuguese colonies. The *Métis* have legal recognition as among the 'Aboriginal peoples of Canada'. In Australia at various times 'mixed-race' or 'half-caste' people have had different or greater legal status and rights than those deemed 'Aborigines' or 'full-bloods'. Some were exempt from restrictive laws that banned Aboriginal people from public swimming pools, cinemas, pubs or schools. Like any government intervention these exemptions could be damaging for families, dividing or segregating people. Yet, when I look at my family in all its mixed beauty, I see that we are a distinct people: not something less 'Indigenous' but certainly unique and born out of the story of Australia.

Being an outsider, something other, reflects our history of exclusion and injustice. My family has suffered through generations, lived at the coalface of bigotry and poverty. I was born into a life on the margins. As I wrote in *Talking to My Country*, we lived in Australia and Australia was for other people. But I have grown from the boy that I was, and my country has grown from the land that it was. Can I truly see privilege as white? Is it black to suffer crippling disadvantage? If these things are true, does this not make me in the eyes of some '*white*'?

Some Indigenous people have begun to explore the impact of this Aboriginal middle class. They recognise it as a phenomenon that is met with suspicion, even hostility, by some in the Indigenous community. Lawyer and academic Professor Larissa Behrendt, in an article for *The Guardian*, 'Who's Afraid of the Indigenous Middle Class?' sees a fracture in Aboriginal communities and politics, between an old guard forged in anger and loyal to the power of protest, and a new generation seeking to work within the system, to join the professions, participate in party politics and seek to make a change.

As she wrote, the fracture seems reflective of so many divisions in Indigenous politics, from opinions about constitutional recognition to disagreements about the nature of welfare reform. While almost everyone can agree on the problems, she writes, the solution causes deep ruptures. She poses critical questions: How does a community that has partly been defined by its exclusion, disadvantage and poverty, redefine itself? How does it increase its participation in the mainstream and not be assimilated? Behrendt ultimately argues that a person's cultural identity should not be tied to poverty. You are not more Aboriginal if you are struggling. But still, suspicion remains. The members of this black middle class are just as likely to be viewed as 'coconuts' – brown on the outside, white on the inside.

In her 2012 series of Boyer Lectures, Professor Marcia Langton, one of Australia's great scholars and an Indigenous woman, tied the growth of an Indigenous middle class to the Australian mining boom of the early 2000s. She conceded that she had had to confront the old trope of Aboriginal people as the hapless victims of a voracious and brutal mining industry. She writes:

Those of us who are successful run the risk of being subject
to abuse, accused of being traitors to our people,
assimilationists and a number of other crimes against the
natural order of things as perceived by those who fail to
understand their inherited racist worldview.

Should a university degree and a job mean that someone is no
longer or less Indigenous? It is ludicrous to suggest that identity
should be means tested. We are free to define ourselves and what
being Indigenous means. The new black middle class is
developing its own consciousness.

From the earliest days of settlement, Aboriginal people
grasped their futures in this new world. A world that brought
devastation, a world they met with fierce resistance and
accommodation. They found a new place in the new economy,
economic migrants in the land of their ancestors. I am of these
people. I was the boy who spent his young years moving from
town to town, as my parents looked for work. I was a part of the
great migration. The descendants of these pioneers are today the
new generation of doctors, lawyers, architects, engineers,
scientists and economists. They are plumbers and carpenters and
electricians and builders. They run small businesses. They are
entrepreneurs and they are redefining what it is to be an
Indigenous person. They overwhelmingly live in our cities and
large towns. They are people who can stand in the Dreaming,
and in the Market.

Everything I am, they have made.

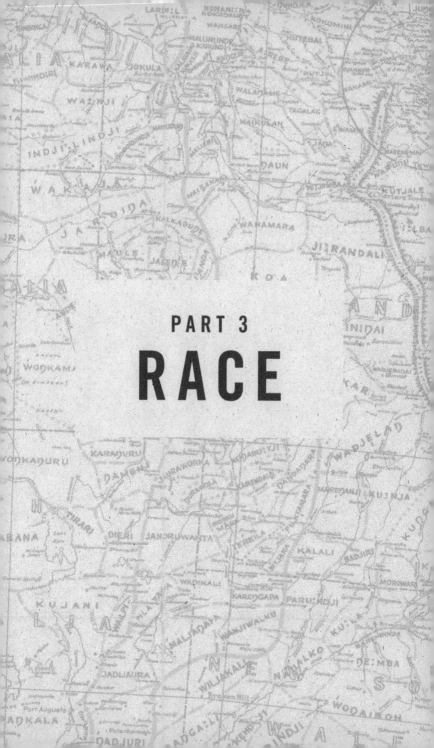

PART 3
RACE

LOOK, A NEGRO!

I must have been about six years old when I first became aware
of colour – my colour – when I first became aware of difference.
That I was marked. That I carried the indelible stain of race. It was
an initiation – an innocent schoolyard initiation – into a world in
which I would be seen through the eyes of others as 'the other'. It
was an incident so ordinary, so playful that if it had happened to
someone else I would likely suspect it was an over-reaction. But it
happened to me and I have never forgotten it. Because I was a
child and the world of a child is small, and because what is
ordinary can loom so large, and because what other children say
matters, and because this came from somewhere, it came from
adults passed down through history, and because nations are
formed from this, and because people are enslaved by this, and
because people are locked up by this, and because of this people
have been lynched, and because people lie about this. And
because I have never forgotten and I am still trying to work it out.
I was damned by my DNA, I carried the gene. I had the one drop
that mattered more than all the other drops.

I had a friend, Owen. He lived in the house behind me. There
was only a fence between us but to me it seemed, at the time, that

he lived in an entirely different world. It was a world apart from mine. He lived in a world where colour blended; where you could even say colour disappeared. It was a world of black and simultaneously of white. It was a home of great love, I remember that. He had six siblings, all of them Aboriginal and all of them adopted. His mother and father were white, the local Presbyterian minister and his wife. They had already had a family; their children were grown and now they had taken on this new brood.

We looked like each other, Owen and me. We could actually see ourselves in each other's faces. At school the teachers would struggle to tell us apart. Perhaps it was simply because we shared the same colour skin; that was probably it. Yes, we were the closest thing to each other and that meant to everyone else we were virtually indistinguishable. Owen and I went to a little school in Coolah, New South Wales; a tiny town, the home of the fabled 'black stump'. Beyond that was the outback, the scary Australian wilderness where people vanished. It was actually part of my ancestral home; Coolah marked the border between my father's people, the Wiradjuri, and my mother's, the Kamilaroi. The Wiradjuri and Kamilaroi, peoples whose names were written over, eliminated from the landscape, foreign to the people who now called this home. Funny isn't it, that the people who lived in Coolah likely never knew that they were speaking another language, that the town took its name from the Kamilaroi word for 'valley of the winds'. Curiously there were no Aboriginal people in the town – only my family and Owen and his siblings – and we were there by default, just another stop on our restless journey. There are old stories that it was bad country; that people fled and never came back. But it is a place that has always been special to me. My childhood memories from there are the most vivid I have.

I started school in Coolah, 1969; five years old, led up the path holding my mother's hand into this new world; a world I was about to discover was so different from my own; a world of whiteness. Each morning we would gather in the school quadrangle and watch the flag being raised. We would recite an oath. 'I honour my God, I serve my Queen, I salute the flag.' It was something that even then, even so young, never felt right. I can still recall that feeling, it was a sense of being displaced, the feeling that I was alone or that everyone else was looking at me. I told my grandfather who lived with us, and he said, 'Cross your fingers, it won't count', so that's what I did. Up would go the flag and I'd place my hands behind me, fingers crossed, my juvenile rebellion.

I was learning the political lessons of life early; already I had a child's sense of being somehow apart. I knew my family was looked upon differently. Aboriginal, that's what we were. But because it was my family, because it was my whole world, I was insulated from the Australia that surrounded me. I hadn't connected myself to the idea of race. In the schoolyard I thought I could be just any other boy. But then that changed – one day, one comment, that framed my world. Tim was one of our best mates. He was the archetypal Aussie kid, I suppose, blond, spiky hair, freckles. Tim was milky white – but then so was Australia. As a nation we were still slowly unravelling the White Australia Policy; it had only been a couple of years since Aboriginal people were finally counted among the Australian population thanks to the 1967 referendum. It has become a recurring joke since – a piece of Aboriginal satire that sounded so right it was mistaken for truth – that we must have been counted among the kangaroos and the wattle, among the flora and fauna.

On this day, Tim put his arm next to Owen's and mine. He looked at his arm and looked again at ours and asked, 'Why are you so black?' Black? Were we really black at all? To be honest, our skin colour probably more resembled the light chocolate-flavoured milk we devoured with such glee each recess. Bottles of chocolate milk warmed by the sun, which we would throw down quickly so that we could get another before the bell rang to go back to class. But black? Black. It wasn't just a colour and it certainly wasn't just a word. No, not a word: it was a world, a world unto its own, a world apart. It was a world to which one was banished. Black was a judgment. Tim, our mate, the boy we sat with in class, kicked a football with, was now looking at us as if for the first time.

Back then, I had no way to respond. There'd be more moments like this to come. Always the feeling was the same, the blood would rush to my cheeks, there would be a flash of anger and then a deep hurt. It was the hurt of being excluded, the hurt of being cast out. And shame, a shame that I was not just different but something less. When it mattered, when all was said and done, I was not one of them. I was on the other side.

'You stupid black prick.' I recall that taunt from the playground.

'Smash the black bastard.' We heard that on the football field.

That was OK, as it went. That was kid's stuff. We could hit back, but we knew we were outnumbered. No matter how defiant, how brave, we could never even the score. They always had reinforcements. But what was worse, what was more damaging, was the judgment from on high. It was the cruel bigotry that set the parameters of our world. It was the school headmaster who told me and some of my black mates that we would never amount to anything. I remember that like a punch in the gut. It was bewildering, even as we joked among ourselves and pretended we didn't care. Alone, I did care, and I know my mates did too.

Tim was the first, and he knew instinctively that he sat in some position of privilege. He knew that he could say to us something we could never say to him; he could tell us we were different. Tim didn't look at Owen and me and say of himself, 'I am so white!' That thought would never occur to him. It would be unthinkable for Tim to imagine that whiteness was in any way unique. To be white was normal. Everything around him was white. Look at all the kids in our class, look at the teacher. White, all of them white. Tim would never have to question himself; this was the unexamined truth of his life: white was not even a colour. White was the origin of light, from which Sir Isaac Newton divined the colour wheel, observing how the colour of light would bend as it passed through the prism. White was purity.

We raced home that day; Owen's mother would always have something for us to eat. She was one of those big-hearted country women, kind and loving. I never thought it strange that he called her Mum. I did know she wasn't what we then called his 'real mum', but she was real to him. In the politics of today, it just wouldn't do, a white couple adopting a crew of black kids. Today, black is supposed to adopt black, to keep the culture. But back then this was a family, and Owen and his siblings were all the better for it. We stood in her kitchen that day, and Owen told her that someone at school had called us black. I didn't say anything. I was a quiet kid, more comfortable observing than speaking. I do so clearly recall what she said next: 'You're not black, you have lovely olive skin.'

There it was. In one day, Owen and I had been called black and then told we were not black. Black was in the eye of the beholder, it was nothing we could own. Tim had spoken the innocence of childhood, but knew more than he realised. Owen's mother had spoken the words of adulthood, the words of politics and power. She was protecting us. She feared what being judged black would mean; she knew that this would be our fate. This day had likely come sooner than she had thought, and if she could keep it at bay for one more day, then she would.

Patrick Wolfe, a historian who has written long and hard about race, once said, 'On a day to day level, race penetrates the most mundane moments of life'. He said when it comes to race, 'we live in a world of mirrors'.

Frantz Fanon, the Algerian writer, knew this all too well. 'I am being dissected under white eyes', he wrote, 'the only real eyes. I am fixed.' As he put it even more starkly: 'Look, a Negro!'

Owen's mum – for all her love – was trapped in the same prism of race as Tim, although Tim pointed out our difference while she sought to deny it. Olive was softer than black. Olive was a suntan. Olive was nearly white. It could never occur to her to say that yes, we were black. She had no words to tell us about our people, about our history, our great victories and triumphs. I wonder if we were Egyptian, would she have told us of the pharaohs and the pyramids? If we were Hawaiian or Tahitian, would that have been more exotic? But no, we were 'black', something to be denied.

This is our education. This is how we learn about race. We learn as we go. We find out about ourselves from children, from teachers, from those who wish to insult us and those who seek to protect us. From the moment a child is born, race lies in wait. It will reveal itself, that much is certain.

THE WHITE GAZE

I discovered James Baldwin when I was thirteen. I stumbled upon his novel *Go Tell It on the Mountain*. It was the title that drew me in. I had always loved the song 'Go Tell It on the Mountain'. Like Baldwin I had a lot of religion in me. Old time religion. Like Baldwin I had been raised in the church – the black church. This was the church of fire and brimstone. This was the church of sin and redemption. We worshipped the sacrificial Jesus of the cross.

Matthew 27:46: 'Eli, Eli, lama sabachthani?' – 'My God, my God, why hast thou forsaken me?'

For we were the forsaken. Ours was the King James Bible – not for us any standardised version – we wanted the sound of the word of God. We loved how the old words rolled around our tongues. My mother would spit my hair down and put me in my best shorts and shirt each Sunday to go to the mission church. My uncle – my father's brother – was the pastor. It was an exalted position in our community – drunks would stand up straighter when he walked by; mothers would silence their kids. My uncle played his role with aplomb. I can still hear him thundering from the pulpit, a handkerchief mopping the sweat from his brow as he pointed at the congregation; we knew he was talking to us.

Luke 17:2: 'It were better for him that a millstone were hanged about his neck, and he cast into the sea, than that he should offend one of these little ones.'

His words hung as heavy as the air. My nausea rising with the heat. My neck stiffening as my temples throbbed. It was all I could do not to flee the church. I knew outside the air was sweet with fruit from the orchards that bordered the mission. The fast-running currents of the irrigation channel promised relief from the swelter, even though the channel could be a foreboding place. It had taken the lives of so many of our people who had fallen in, drunk. The channel was guarded by a blanket of sharp-edged burrs – catheads we called them – jagged vicious things that once piercing the skin would burn for hours.

Cooped in that little wooden church with my uncle's shout and spit I would risk it all to run. But of course I couldn't escape my mother's eye – she would cast me sideways disapproving glances when she sensed my irritation growing.

The hymns we sang were old and forlorn.

'The Old Rugged Cross'. 'Amazing Grace'. 'Shall We Gather at the River'.

Soon we'll reach the silver river,
Soon our pilgrimage will cease,
Soon our happy hearts will quiver
With the melody of peace.

All of these songs promised a better day – because a better day was all we could hope for. These days of sermon and song prepared me for James Baldwin. *Go Tell It on the Mountain* was the story he had to tell. It was his life in the church. It was his life among his people. It was the story of two brothers, John and Roy, and their father the preacher – histories hidden, bodies buried and children left to untangle a family's secrets. This was the world slavery made. It came out of the black American experience but it spoke powerfully to me.

To an Aboriginal boy moving on the margins of outback New South Wales, poor and itinerant but in love with books and words, Baldwin sounded like home. We were living in a world that could not see us and Baldwin made me visible. Before Baldwin, books were entertainment. I spent many hours with Mark Twain, Robert Louis Stevenson, Charles Dickens, Arthur Conan Doyle. My mother would scrounge books wherever she could. I don't recall much in the way of birthday or Christmas presents – a scooter and a bike stand out – but I devoured my most treasured gift, a book of Greek myths. I was transported to the world of Icarus and Narcissus and Zeus.

But Baldwin fixed me in the firmament – the place between worlds, separating the waters of the white and the waters of the black. Here was a place for me. Here was a writer of courage and truth. The people of his book arrived fully formed, they didn't exist as a reflection of whiteness, this wasn't blackness as imagined, but real and flawed and courageous and pitiful. People who surprised and disappointed. These were people – black people – who were human.

Baldwin said, 'I wish only to be an honest man and a good writer.'

He was both.

A black man confronting his country's legacy of racism. A son confronting his father's hypocrisy. A gay man confronting his sexuality. Through his exploration of identity and belonging he became a touchstone for me. After *Go Tell It on the Mountain*, I devoured whatever I could find. His essays were searing meditations on race and history. Each line quotable and a lesson in life. Words so brutally rendered that they make me wince even now. Words now unutterable, almost unthinkable.

'For the state, a nigger is a nigger is a nigger ... sometimes Mr or Mrs or Dr Nigger.'

They speak to the America of Black Lives Matter, the America that questioned the citizenship of Barack Obama, as powerfully as they spoke to the Jim Crow segregated south of Baldwin's time.

Baldwin said that he had to learn to navigate this world that so controlled him, he had to learn to 'outwit white people' in order to survive. This was my world too. How to navigate a world where I was always underestimated, trapped by the tyranny of low expectations? I knew what he meant when he wrote that fear 'rose up like a wall between the world and me'. Baldwin gave voice to what I knew but could not say. On the centenary of the emancipation proclamation – the freeing of the slaves – Baldwin wrote *The Fire Next Time*, a letter to his nephew, his brother's son:

> I know what the world has done to my brother and how
> narrowly he has survived it. And I know, which is much
> worse, and this is the crime of which I accuse my country
> and my countrymen, and for which neither I nor time nor
> history will ever forgive them, that they have destroyed and
> are destroying hundreds of thousands of lives and do not
> know it and do not want to know it.

I have returned so often to Baldwin, his work has been a touchstone throughout my life. I have often disagreed with him – at his worst there is a nihilism that I could never embrace – yet he has never been less than captivating. In post-Obama America, a new generation of black writers have turned to Baldwin once again. When I read his words I feel their weight. They are as sharp, as penetrating today as when I first encountered them. What a world they reveal; the tragedy of so many lives laid waste. I turned to Baldwin when I heard the news that another Indigenous child had taken her life. She was only ten years old, living in a remote northwestern corner of Western Australia. Ten years old – we know what that looks like, what that should look like. Ten years old should be giggling at the back of the school bus. Ten years old should be swapping notes behind the teacher's back in class. Ten years old should be singing into a hairbrush and dancing in front of a mirror. But ten years old to this girl looked like hopelessness. This would be shocking if it were rare … but for Australia's First Peoples this is so numbingly familiar. Indigenous kids under the age of fourteen are almost ten times more likely to kill themselves than their non-Indigenous counterparts.

I turned again to Baldwin when we as a nation heard the screams of Aboriginal boys locked up and beaten. James Baldwin – so unflinching, so unbowed a man writing free of the white gaze. I turned again to *The Fire Next Time*:

> You were born into a society which spelled out with brutal
> clarity, and in as many ways as possible, that you were a
> worthless human being.

Those words are so harsh that they are brutal, and there are times I want to recoil. While I have been inspired by Baldwin, angered by Baldwin, saddened by Baldwin, I have struggled with his certainty. Race is such a part of our lives, it so defines us that it can be hard to imagine an escape. But does it answer everything? The United States, a country that once held people in bondage, went to war with itself to free those same slaves. White boys gave their lives for the freedom of others. The Civil War is still the determining moment in that nation's history, a blood vow that, in the words of Abraham Lincoln at Gettysburg, 'These dead shall not have died in vain – that this nation, under God, shall have a new birth of freedom.'

Doesn't my life tell me that race is not a prison? Unlike Baldwin, I look for the spaces in between, those questions that defy easy answers. My instinct is to soften the blow. Even knowing what I know I struggle to accept that my country should be condemned by the worst of its history. Are we – black people – still in Baldwin's words 'worthless'? Is this my country? Today, at this time, is this who we are? I think of my fellow Australians of goodwill – those who have loved and cried with us – and I say surely this, the better angels of our nature, is the true measure of us.

But then I think again how 97 per cent of kids locked up in the Northern Territory are black kids. I think of their parents too likely to have been behind bars. I think of their grandparents likely gone too soon, dead before their time. In this country Indigenous people die ten years younger than other Australians. I think of how suicide remains the single biggest cause of death for Indigenous people under the age of thirty-five. I think of Aboriginal women, forty-five times more likely to suffer domestic violence than their white sisters. An Aboriginal woman is more than ten times more likely to be killed from violent assault.

I think of lives chained to generations of misery.

To write about this is confronting. I have to cast aside any self-doubt; to care more for what I want to say than how people might react. We are vulnerable when we write; but we must be ready to risk rejection or condemnation, if we are to write free of what has been called 'the white gaze'. The white gaze – it is a phrase that resonates in black American literature. Writers from W.E.B. Du Bois to Ralph Ellison to Baldwin and Toni Morrison have struggled with it and railed against it. As Morrison – a Nobel Laureate – once said:

> Our lives have no meaning, no depth without the white
> gaze. And I have spent my entire writing life trying to make
> sure that the white gaze was not the dominant one in any of
> my books.

The white gaze: it traps black people in white imaginations. It is the eyes of a white schoolteacher who sees a black student and lowers expectations. It is the eyes of a white cop who sees a black person and looks twice – or worse, feels for a gun. Du Bois explored this more than a century ago in his book *The Souls of Black Folk*, reflecting on his conversations with white people and the ensuing delicate dance around the 'Negro problem'.

> Between me and the other world there is an ever unasked
> question ... All, nevertheless, flutter around it ... Instead of
> saying directly, how does it feel to be a problem? They say, I

> know an excellent coloured man in my town.... To the real
> question ... I answer seldom a word.

The flame has passed to a new generation. In recent years I have
looked to three more black writers who have stared down the
white gaze. In their own ways Ta-Nehisi Coates, Claudia Rankine
and George Yancy have held up a mirror to white America. These
are uncompromising and fearless voices. Coates' searing book-
length essay *Between The World And Me* critiques America
against a backdrop of black deaths at the hands of police. He says
the country's history is rooted in slavery and the assault against
the black body. In the form of a letter to his son, Coates writes:

> Here is what I would like for you to know: In America it is
> traditional to destroy the black body – it is heritage.

In *Citizen – An American Lyric*, poet Rankine reflects on the
black experience from the victims of Hurricane Katrina, to
Trayvon Martin, a seventeen-year-old black youth shot dead by a
Neighbourhood Watch volunteer who was acquitted, to black
tennis star Serena Williams. In each case Rankine sees lives
framed by whiteness. She writes:

> because white men can't
> police their imagination
> black men are dying

Philosophy professor George Yancy penned an article for the
New York Times in 2015, a letter he addressed to 'Dear White
America'. Yancy asked his countrymen and women to listen with

love, and to look at those things, he said, that might cause pain and terror. 'All white people,' he said, 'benefit from racism and this means each, in their own way, are racist.

'... don't run to seek shelter from your own racism ... practise being vulnerable. Being neither a "good" white person, nor a liberal white person will get you off the proverbial hook.'

Yancy's letter was not tempered by the fact a black man was in the White House; that only made voices like his more urgent. Coates, Rankine, Yancy, each has been variously praised and awarded, yet each has been pilloried as well. This is inevitable when some people don't like what the mirror reflects.

It takes courage for a person defined and judged as black to speak to a white world; a world that can render invisible people of colour, unless they begin to more closely resemble white people themselves: an education, a house in the suburbs, a good job, lighter skin. In Australia, too, black voices are defying the white gaze. We may not have the popular cut-through of a Morrison or a Baldwin or a Coates, but we have a proud tradition – Oodgeroo Noonuccal, Kevin Gilbert, Ruby Ginibi Langford and more recently Kim Scott, Alexis Wright, Anita Heiss. Their styles and genres are many and varied but there is a common and powerful theme of defiance and survival.

This is a world so instantly recognisable to us – Indigenous people – but still so foreign to white Australia. I think of Natalie Harkin's book of poetry, *Dirty Words*, a subversive dictionary that turns English words back on their users. A is apology, B is boat people ... on and on ... G is for genocide ... S for sovereignty.

'How do you dream,' she writes, 'when your Lucky-Country does not sleep?'

Bruce Pascoe's award-winning *Dark Emu* challenges the white stereotype of the 'primitive hunter-gatherer'. He says the economy and culture of Indigenous people has been grossly undervalued. He cites journals and diaries of explorers and colonists to reveal the industry and ingenuity of pre-colonial Aboriginal society. He says it is a window into a world of people building dams and wells and houses, irrigating and harvesting seed and creating elaborate cemeteries.

Tony Birch is an acclaimed novelist, whose *Ghost River* is remarkable. It is the story of two friends navigating the journey into adulthood, guided by the men of the river; men others may see as homeless and hopeless. It is a work infused with a sense of place and belonging. Ellen van Neerven – someone I have mentioned earlier – is one of the most exciting young writers in our country. She challenges comfortable notions of identity: sexual, racial and national. Her writing is provocative and challenging and mind bending, and altogether stunning.

I share a kinship with these writers, even if, like Baldwin, I don't always share their world-view. A nation is its stories, and these are stories that shake our confidence. That these works are not more widely read is a national shame.

George Yancy asks white Americans to become 'un-sutured', to open themselves up and let go of their white innocence. The same could be said here. That it is past time that we truly knew each other. Why is this important? Well, for white people it may simply be a matter of choice, the fate of black people may not directly affect them. For others it is survival; the white gaze means people die young, are locked up and locked out of work and education.

When I come to write, I still come with Baldwin as my guide. I come to write free of the white gaze yet aware too that to understand myself, to understand my country, is to understand how we are all bound by race.

I am born of deep traditions. My footprints trace the first steps on this land. I am born too of the white imagination – this imagination that said we did not exist. The imagination that said this was an empty land – terra nullius. It is not just a legal doctrine, it is a state of mind. We were rendered invisible, our rights extinguished. If we existed at all, we were just as likely dismissed as the fly-blown savages unfit to be counted among the civilised races of the earth. The story here was a story written in other lands; a story of colonisation, subjugation, invasion, disease, death, dispossession. As Canadian political scientist Joyce Green has written:

> The dehumanisation of indigenous peoples was necessary
> for dispossession and subsequent judicial oppression.

Dispossession and oppression, the white gaze that justified or could turn a blind eye to the ravages of massacre and disease that devastated my people. It was the white gaze of settlers that left some of my ancestors dead on the plains. It was the white gaze that left no place for us in this new nation. It was the white gaze that at the time of Federation forecast our doom, a race bound for extinction and not fit to be counted among the citizens of this country.

We hear the white gaze in the words of our second prime minister, Alfred Deakin:

> We have power to deal with people of any and every race
> within our borders, except the aboriginal inhabitants of the

continent, who remain under the custody of the States.
There is that single exception of a dying race; and if they are
a dying race, let us hope that in their last hours they will be
able to recognise not simply the justice, but the generosity of
the treatment which the white race, who are dispossessing
them and entering into their heritage, are according them.

Think about that. That we would die out and that we would be
grateful for small mercies. By the time I was born in 1963 the
white gaze had placed us on the margins of society, on the outside
looking in. My parents' lives had been singed by the fires of
bigotry and poverty. We moved from town to town, my father
having little to offer but his muscle and his willingness to work.

I have wondered how people, comfortable in their place in
Australia, would have looked upon me as a child: a dozen schools
before I was in my teens, no permanent home, an itinerant labourer
father, a gypsy caravan of extended family, born black and poor.
Would they have argued I would be better removed from those
who loved me? Yet this same family raised me from sawmill shacks
to stand in the oval office at the White House and the Great Hall of
the People in Beijing. My journey has taken me around the world.

I found a personal liberation in countries torn by their own
histories yet where I could walk free of mine. I am of my people –
the First People of this land – yet I have lived far from them. I
have made a life – a good life – in an Australia that still struggles
to acknowledge the rights of those people I call my own. It is a
contradiction, a maddening contradiction, that race alone cannot
resolve. It is a reason that true peace often feels just out of reach.
It is the restlessness of someone in between, who can at times
find belonging suffocating; someone neither black nor white.

Surely to be free of the white gaze is to simply write free. I must be free too of the black gaze; my writing allows me to explore identity but not to be limited by it. It is why I cannot accept those who tell me to 'stay in my lane'. I have never been convinced by the argument that only black people can write about the black experience or that I could not imagine a white life. The same goes for any *identity* group: racial, religious, sexual or gender. What is a black writer? Why should we assume that every writer of colour will share the same experience or world view? Writing – any art – is a deeply human experience and I could not possibly divide or privilege one part of myself against another. To be trapped in identity for me would be a creative and intellectual death. My life has been enriched by reading what some now deride as 'old white men'. How would Shakespeare have written *Othello*, if his whiteness precluded him from writing of blackness? Thomas Keneally has said he would not now write *The Chant of Jimmie Blacksmith*, yet what is that book if not an intensely Australian story? The story of a man both black and white, defined by race at the birth of a new nation, became a touchstone for me as a boy. Writing is inextricably political and the 'white gaze' has obliterated or marginalised blackness, but once free why would I swap one prison for another? Those Indigenous writers who speak to the black experience are white as well – like me – so which part of our humanity do we seek to suppress? Toni Morrison, a writer who as much as anyone has stared down the white gaze, has said, 'My work requires me to think about how free I can be as an African-American woman writer in my genderised, sexualised, wholly racialised world.'

I come from a long line of storytellers – I look to the world of poets not politics. Poetry is the world of deeper truths, truth that must not be bound by political ideas of identity. As the poet John Keats said, 'a poet is the most unpoetical of anything in existence, because he has no identity'. As always, for me there is James Baldwin. In this time of heightened race politics, so many are looking back to Baldwin, yet are often guilty of seeing the Baldwin they wish to see. I look to the James Baldwin who wrote, 'Each of us, helplessly and forever, contains the other – male in female, female in male, white in black and black in white. We are a part of each other.'

I came across an article in the *New York Times*, remembering Baldwin, and again I was reminded of how this writer from another time and another country spoke so much of what I feel. How race, for all that it seeks to define us, for all that others cling to it, is a straitjacket. It suffocates and strangles us. That there is a white gaze is true; but we can be trapped in the judgment of our own, those who would revel in race and tell us what to think, who to love or who to be. As Baldwin said, those who are quick to say, 'You are acting white.' Baldwin reminded me again that we are all trapped in the vicious, twisted logic of race.

> I was a maverick, a maverick in the sense that I depended on neither the white world nor the black world. That was the only way I could've played it. I would've been broken otherwise. I had to say, 'A curse on both your houses.' The fact that I went to Europe so early is probably what saved me. It gave me another touchstone — myself.

Myself: I am black – uniquely and deeply black. But my *blackness* cannot be separated from that part of me that is white; that is my gaze – a world beyond certainty and closer to freedom.

THE AUSTRALIAN VOICE

What is the 'Australian voice'? It's an odd question. I am not sure what an Australian is let alone what is its voice. For much of my life, an Australian identity has sat somewhere out of reach. I was something else, something we call Indigenous. Even that word itself is a trap, an identity constructed by someone else, within which I am meant to find myself. There have been other words: Aborigines, Aboriginals, Abos ... and worse, much worse, that don't warrant repeating.

Sometimes, even though we share a language, we can completely misunderstand each other. For Aboriginal people, language has become a feature of loss. It was part of our invisibility; how who we were was extinguished. The names the first people of this land gave to their country remain largely unknown to most Australians; lost even to some Indigenous people. This is living with terra nullius: empty land. Where are the people?

Perhaps this is the Australian voice; the voice of terra nullius, the voice of empty spaces. Indigenous people know that voice ... it was the voice of the frontier, the voices of settlers. Listen to them, taken from the pages of our history books, from the newspapers of nineteenth-century Australia.

Is there room for both of us here? No. Then the sooner the weaker is wiped out the better as we may save some valuable lives in the process.

Any doubt, therefore, as to the lawfulness of our assuming the possession of this island, must arise from the opinion that it was the property of it original inhabitants. Such opinion, however, would be incorrect; for the very notion of property, as applicable to territorial possession did not exist among them.

We know the Australian voice; it was written into the constitution:

In reckoning the numbers of the people of the Commonwealth, or of a State or other part of the Commonwealth, aboriginal natives shall not be counted.

Yes, the Australian voice we heard was the voice of exclusion. It was also the voices of doom: the prophets of extinction. Voices, like our second prime minister Alfred Deakin.

When we became a nation, the Australian voice, as Deakin heard it, was only ever imagined as the voice of whiteness.

A white Australia does not by any means mean only the preservation of the complexion of the people of this country. It means the multiplying of their homes, so that we may be able to occupy, use and defend every part of our continent; it means the maintenance of the conditions of life fit for white men and white women.

Of course we have changed, haven't we? Or is this the Australian voice?

> The push for globalisation, economic rationalism, free trade
> and ethnic diversity has seen our country's decline. This is
> due to the foreign takeover of our land ... Australia had a
> national identity before federation and it had nothing to do
> with diversity ... If you are not prepared to become
> Australian, respect our culture and way of life then I suggest
> you go back to where you came from.

Yes, Pauline Hanson speaks for a minority, we keep telling ourselves that. But what, then, were all those senators doing lining up to hug her after her parliamentary speech?

Our constitution has changed. The 1967 referendum meant Aboriginal people were finally counted, finally included in the census. But still we are seen as a people apart, Australians but different.

I am reminded of the words of the Nobel Prize-winning poet Czeslaw Milosz, to the world considered Polish, but in fact Lithuanian. 'I am a Lithuanian to whom it was not given to be a Lithuanian,' he wrote. Perhaps this is my fate, am I an Australian to whom it was not given to be an Australian? Milosz lived within the sliding doors of identity, born and raised Catholic in rural Lithuania. He spoke Polish, Russian, English and French, yet not a word of Lithuanian. Later in life, he hired a Lithuanian language coach. Language, he said, 'is the only homeland'.

My father says the same thing; he says language tells us not just who we are but where we are. He is a wise man; it is wisdom that comes from the certainty of being. He is a Wiradjuri man, born and raised on his country, the country on which he lives still. I have never known my father to have a crisis of identity. To him, being Wiradjuri is as natural as breathing. My father has language that speaks to his sense of place. The birds, the rocks, the trees, the hills and the waters have names that echo through millennia. To hear these words fall from his tongue is to know who he is and where he is.

'Balladhu Wiradjuri gibir. Dyirramadilinya badhu Wiradjuri: I am a Wiradjuri man – proudly Wiradjuri.'

My father can speak those words with unflinching belief. There is no dissonance between word and man and place. In a country of many tongues that speak of other lands, who can say this? I am who I am and I am from here. It is a certainty I don't quite possess; that I don't seek to possess. My life has been lived in the worlds in between. If language tells us not who we are but where we are, then who am I? Where am I, when my language is English? I have made my life, my career, out of a love of the English language. I have had a lifelong passion for words and books. I love the rhythm and the musical quality of a beautifully constructed sentence. This is the language of Shakespeare. Who could not find the divine in the bard's sonnets?

If I could write the beauty of your eyes,
And in fresh numbers number all your graces,
The age to come would say 'This poet lies;
Such heavenly touches ne'er touched earthly faces.'

This is the language that set loose the imagination of Bob Dylan. It is the language of the rock music rebellion that I so identified with: Jimi Hendrix, The Rolling Stones, Led Zeppelin, The Clash, the Sex Pistols, The Jam and The Smiths. It is the language of the great writers who have shaped my life and ideas.

My travels have opened up a world of languages and the people who speak them. My closest friend overseas was an Iranian cameraman steeped in Persian poetry. My Pakistani friends introduced me to the music of Nusrat Fateh Ali Khan. I had no need of interpretation to feel the power of his words. I have the same feeling listening to the Tuareg rock band Tinariwen.

Other languages have words that speak with a force that eludes their English equivalent. The Arabic word for justice – *adl* – means to put things in order, to return to their rightful place. That has always felt more profound to me than our Western ideas of fairness, equity or objectivity. I love how dissident Chinese, their thoughts and words monitored and censored by the Communist Party, play with language and exploit ambiguous meaning. When I lived in Beijing, I became a fan of the underground rock band Carsick Cars, who had a song called *Zhong Nan Hai* – at once the name of the official residence and headquarters of the party leadership and a brand of cigarettes.

Being exposed to new languages, meeting different people, understanding how they see and express their world and the world around them has enriched me. These friendships have made me a better person. I can speak some Chinese, some Arabic and some French. I will spend my lifetime struggling and failing to master English. But in truth, Wiradjuri – the language of my father – was never a big part of my life. As a boy it wasn't spoken, the old people kept their silence. We fashioned a patois – a creole mix of Wiradjuri and English. We had words for white people and police and food and animals; it was a language apart, it belonged to us, likely incomprehensible to others. But it wasn't Wiradjuri. It was a language like us – people clinging to often shattered traditions, part of an old world and not yet finding a place in the new. Yes, language tells us not just who we are but where we are.

This Australia had supplanted us. Our languages fell silent as surely as our people were forced from our lands and herded onto reserves and missions, our lives controlled. My father's grandfather was arrested and locked up after police overheard him speaking Wiradjuri to his grandson in the streets of his hometown. Now my father has kept faith with his grandfather. The old man's language is spoken again. My father is teaching Wiradjuri to a new generation.

To some Indigenous people recovering language is like recovering self. They see it not just as reasserting their blackness but rejecting whiteness. Some reclaim or create 'traditional' names, reaching back to an ancestral past that to them, feels more authentic than the names of the colonisers they were born with. Here is the struggle for identity of a people whose identities have been defined – indeed legislated – by others, with often devastating personal cost. Just who is and what is Aboriginal remains contested. Language and names are markers of identity. This is how we introduce ourselves to the world; how we explain ourselves to each other. I admire this conscious effort to keep themselves and their people alive in the world, but I am wary too. I am who I am and I am born of a country whose history is what it is. My struggle is to live free, to determine my identity unconstrained by the expectations or definitions of others, white or black.

Reviving Indigenous languages is in itself a response to a history of oppression and denial. It can be liberating and assertive, but like all identity it is a construction. Identity – to me – is not a singular thing. My life's journey has added new layers to who I am. Inspired by my father and to honour his legacy and the traditions of our people I have learned more of the Wiradjuri language. I am proud when I see my children, raised in China and the Middle East as much as Australia, finding pride in being Wiradjuri.

Sometimes we must free ourselves from language as surely as we must free ourselves of our families, our countries. The Chinese-American writer, Yiyun Li, writes in English to forget Chinese. She says, 'the intimacy between one and one's mother tongue can be comforting and irreplaceable, yet it can also demand more than one is willing to give, or more than one is capable of giving'. Chinese language she equates with oppression and the heavy hand of the state; freedom and liberation come with renouncing the language and the Communist Party. The absoluteness of her abandonment of Chinese, she says, is 'a kind of suicide'.

Yiyun Li says, 'language is capable of sinking a mind. One's thoughts are slavishly bound to language.' This may explain why some Aboriginal people reclaim their ancestral languages; it represents more than just revival: it is a form of survival. Yet English is my first language – in truth my only language. To learn Wiradjuri is like learning Chinese, or French or Italian; I can speak the words but never truly hold the thoughts. That may be my loss, but in English I find the words to describe myself.

THE VOODOO OF RACE

Like millions of us, in 2018 I watched the royal wedding; our family put aside the usual cynicism and made a night of it. My sister-in-law was visiting from Hawaii, she came over to our house with my mother-in-law and her partner. There we were, me an Indigenous Australian with my non-Indigenous wife; her sister whose late husband was an Indigenous Hawaiian and who is now married to a Filipino; their mother whose partner of 30 years is a New Zealand Maori. A modern multi-ethnic mixed family watching a so-called mixed – half-black–half-white – American actress, Meghan Markle, marry a British 'blue blood' prince.

The scene revealed how in so many ways the whole concept of race is flawed, yet for that moment it seemed the world was fixated on it. The royal wedding commentary returned to it time and again, as the bride was referred to as 'mixed race' or 'biracial'. One British commentator, part of the ABC's coverage, even wondered ridiculously about the future children of Meghan and Harry who, in her words, could be 'all sorts of colours'.

Race is a strange subject. Race is a lie. I know that now. In fact it is worse than a lie. It is voodoo, it is witchcraft. Race owes as much to science as the evil eye. Yet, just like witchcraft, we believe it. We give race its power. The crops in the field failed, why? Because Annie Smith is a witch, I saw her dancing at midnight around a fire, yelling obscene incantations. And so the local villagers turn on her. They ostracise her. Her family is banished. Her house burned to the ground. Is medieval fantasy any different from the idea that someone can be lynched, hung from a tree, set alight because that person is what is deemed to be black? Was that person lynched because of his colour? Consider this: a young black girl is ordered out of a swimming pool because the other children have complained. Is it because of her colour? No, it is because of what people *believed* about her colour.

Somewhere in human history, we gave colour power. There was something in the hue of skin, the kink of hair, the width of a nose or the prominence of a brow ridge that we believed determined a person's character. Colour was immutable. Colour was permanent. In America one drop was all it took, one drop of blood, one black ancestor in a tangled family tree, and forever that person was black. A white mother could give birth to a black child, but was it conceivable that a black mother would give birth to a white child? Never. Black was what white wasn't; it was the anti-white; it was opposite. It was the dark side. There it is in our language: blackmail, blacken a name, blackguard, the black sheep of the family. Why is it the white knight who comes to the damsel's rescue?

Race crept in under the cover of science. It held sway for hundreds of years, from the 1600s to the mid-twentieth century, enough time to lodge itself deep into our consciousness. Just spend a moment searching references to science and racism, immediately there are images of skulls, an evolutionary chart supposedly tracking the progress of man from dark to light. Phrenology was the science of measuring skulls, feeling for bumps, from which intelligence supposedly could be deduced.

Who could argue with race, didn't it come from the Bible? *Blackness* was the curse of Canaan. Canaan was the son of Ham, condemned by his father Noah. Like so many biblical stories it is open to interpretation, but Ham was said to have witnessed Noah drunk and naked, some religious scholars believe there was a sexual transgression. Canaan and his descendants would pay the price, forever to be the 'servant of servants'. It was seized on to justify slavery and racism.

Here is how race begins, in fear and superstition: pseudo-science and distorted readings of the Bible. Race is a hydra, its many heads giving it different forms. I am something that is considered black in Australia, yet in other parts of the world I would be seen as white. History, time, place, these are the things that shape our ideas of race. Race exists in the eye of the beholder; just like magic what we *believe* we *see*. Black can be whatever we want it to be, Jews have been 'black'; Irish, Greeks, Italians have been 'black'. Funny thing, the more familiar we become – the closer we get to *white* – the less black we are. I have lost count of the number of times someone has said to me that I am *not really black!*

Race as an idea gained power in what we call the Enlightenment, the seventeenth-century philosophical revolution of thought that sought to liberate us from superstition, to demolish hierarchy, to elevate reason and bind us to a universal humanity where the individual was freed from the bonds of tribe. As Immanuel Kant wrote, 'Enlightenment is man's emergence from self-imposed nonage.' Enlightenment was freedom; if it had a motto it was 'dare to know'.

Yet the age of reason was also the age of discovery; race became a justification for colonisation. Rousseau spoke of the rights of man, but pseudo-science – the belief that there was a genetic hierarchy of colour – spoke of the exception of blackness. Together these two ideas animated the world. As Patrick Wolfe says, 'Race reconciled the great taxonomies of natural science with the political rhetoric of the rights of man.' We divided ourselves by race, we enslaved people by race; we dispossessed people by race; race defined power: the more *white*, the more *powerful*. As Wolfe, writes, race was applied 'with the fixity of a curse'.

The truth is we belong to one human family, and advances in the study of DNA show we all draw our heritage from different parts of the globe. In this way, we are all 'mixed'. As geneticist David Reich, says in his recent book *Who We Are and How We Got Here*, 'the genome revolution – turbo charged by ancient DNA – has revealed that human populations are related to each other in ways that no one expected.' Humans have followed the same winding path out of Africa, the fossil evidence and now the genetic research connects us to our 'ancestral Eve'.

Historian Barbara Fields and her sister, sociologist Karen Fields have dissected this thing we call race in their book, *Racecraft*. The Fields sisters, who are what we would classify as African-American, say race deflects attention from racism. Disguised as race, they say, racism becomes something African Americans are, rather than something racists do. Race is superstition, it belongs to the same family as witchcraft, but *racism*, they say, 'belongs to the same family as murder and genocide'.

The Fields sisters ask us to look beyond race; to untangle ourselves from its pernicious twisted logic; to abandon the language of race. This is easier said than done. It extends beyond race. Gender, sexuality, class, politics: all of it seeks to define us and separate us. Ideas of 'race' have brought out the worst of humanity. They have inspired – and continue to inspire – genocide, holocaust, war, dispossession, colonisation, imperialism, slavery, lynchings, segregation, mass incarceration.

Personally and individually 'race' ties us in knots. Meghan Markle's mother is considered black and her father white. Until very recently, America's 'one drop' rule – one drop of 'black blood' – made Meghan too, black. The American census now allows people to self-identify, in ever more convoluted and exotic abstractions and hyphens. The golfer Tiger Woods has gone to ludicrous linguistic lengths to describe himself, inventing his own category 'Cablinasian' to reflect his Caucasian, Black, Indian, Asian roots. Meghan Markle, in an op-ed for *Elle* magazine, wrote of how she has embraced 'the gray area surrounding my self-identification, keeping me with a foot on both sides of the fence'.

Race has us trapped. It is all but impossible for us to think about ourselves or articulate a sense of identity without referring to race. I identify as an Indigenous Australian; it is something deeply personal, arising from an enduring connection to Indigenous heritage in my mother's and father's families. Historically we have been categorised as 'Aboriginal' or 'Indigenous' or more colloquially or disparagingly as the 'blacks'. That has meant at various times being subject to government policy that has restricted our liberty; has told us where we could live and who we could marry. Families have been divided on arbitrary rulings of colour. The Australian Law Reform Commission lists historically sixty-four different definitions of who was considered as Indigenous.

Let me tell you about my grandmother. She lived a life on the margins; locked out in segregated 1930s Australia. She was turned away from hospital when she was giving birth to her first child; she watched as the police bulldozed to the ground the tiny humpy she called home leaving her and her children destitute. She was harassed and ostracised. She experienced the full weight of the darkest periods of Australian racism. My grandmother was white. Yes, she lived with an Aboriginal man, had black children, and her stepfather and half-brother were black. But she was white. If being Aboriginal is about a history of exclusion and discrimination, of oppression and brutality, my grandmother would have had a far greater claim on that identity than me.

Today I am asked to tick a box on the census form identifying whether I am Aboriginal. It is an entirely invented category that erases the complexity of my heritage. I am descended from Wiradjuri and Kamilaroi people but I also have an Irish convict ancestor and my maternal grandmother was European; how can that census box possibly contain all of me? How can I tick a box that excludes my grandmother? Why is my son asked to tick a box that his mother cannot? See how quickly we become bogged in the swamp of scientifically meaningless racial categorisation: was my grandmother 'white'? My grandfather 'black'? What race could properly describe me?

None of us are 'pure'. Yet the politics of 'whiteness' means it is often normalised and 'blackness' seen as something 'other'. These are relationships of power not science. Can we be truly post-racial? This was the tantalising possibility raised by the election in 2008 of Barack Obama, a man with a white mother and a black Kenyan father, as American president. His election was hailed as the fulfilment of the Martin Luther King Jnr promise of being judged not by colour but character. The writer Touré challenged the whole idea of 'blackness' in his book *Who's Afraid of Post-Blackness?* He said, 'the point of fighting for freedom is for black folk to define blackness as we see fit.' As he made clear, there are forty million blacks in America and forty million ways to be black.

America is consumed by race, in ways that I have found nowhere else. I remember visiting with my sons, each of them different shades of colour. My youngest son was greeted everywhere in Spanish – mistaken for a Mexican – and his brother would regularly receive a nod of recognition and solidarity from African-Americans. Here is the folly of race, that people in the same family can be categorised on sight so very differently.

Historian and social scientist David Hollinger has called for Americans to 'push yet harder against the authority that shape and colour have historically been allowed by society to exert over our culture'. Hollinger, in his book *Postethnic America*, dismisses the idea of 'fixed' identities; he favours making room for new communities that promote solidarity between people beyond definitions of race or ethnicity. As he says, we 'live in an age not of identities but affiliations'.

It is a worthy notion that remains a work in progress. America is far from being a 'post-racial' nation. The election of Donald Trump is seen critically as a return to old hardened attitudes of racial prejudice and a victory for white supremacy. Ta-Nehisi Coates has called Trump 'the first white President'. The Trump ideology, Coates says, 'is white supremacy in all of its truculent and sanctimonious power'. Yet Coates, for all the power and eloquence of his writing, is himself caught in the racial bind: railing against it yet defined by it. The same may be said of me.

To Coates America is irredeemably racist; it is, he says, 'heritage'; it is 'tradition'. America, he has written, is built on the plunder of black bodies. What troubles me so about this? Could I not look to Australia and see a story of wealth extracted from Aboriginal suffering? Yes. And yet, it is a bleak world that cannot imagine hope or progress. Coates himself has said it is not his job to offer hope. Yet hope has kept me alive and it was hope that delivered Barack Obama to the White House: the 'audacity of hope'. White voters who would eventually turn to Donald Trump, for a moment believed enough in America's promise to elect a black man to the presidency.

Obama spoke of a 'nation where all things are possible', yet reality has a habit of mugging hope. As the historian Gary Gerstle points out:

> If Obama's election produced spasms of racial vertigo, the
> reality for millions of African-Americans who cheered his
> victory, continued to be contoured by the very forces of
> racial segregation, police brutality, poverty, unemployment
> that in some quarters, Obama's election had suddenly made
> irrelevant.

Race matters, even if the evidence tells us it should not. Shifting our language is not some 'Kumbaya', all-hold-hands fantasy; it is urgent: race exacts a terrible human toll. Barbara and Karen Fields, remind us that 'race is the principle unit and core concept of racism'. Racism, they write, is a social practice that 'always takes for granted the objective reality of race'. *Racecraft* turns the consequence – colour – into the cause. *Racecraft* switches the burden of blame: an individual is discriminated against because they are perceived as black, not because of anything inherent in the shade of their skin, but entirely because enough people have acted on their ideas of colour. It is racism that is the parent of race, not the other way around.

The Fields sisters say that we have moved beyond fears of witchcraft, but racecraft persists. They reject the language of race, even terms like 'mixed-race' or 'post-racialism': these draw from the same well as racism. As they write, 'restoring notions of race mixture to centre stage recommits us, willy-nilly, to the discredited idea of racial purity, the basic premise of bio-racism'. That's what all the discussion about Meghan Markle's 'race' was really doing – perpetuating voodoo science and fuelling the same old fears of difference, as if that has not done enough damage to our world already.

WOEGRA
UGARINJIN
GUIDJ
WOLJAMIDI
MIRIWUN
NGARINMAN
KWARA
WALADJADARI
DJERAG
WANDJIRA
MUDBARA
TJII
NORTHERN

WARWA
KONEJANDJI
LUDJA
GIDJA
(INI)
BIGONGINA
WA

DJARU
MADJALA
IJIKENA

WULUMARI
BUNA:RA
JULBRE
GOGODA

WAIADARA
WALMALA
WALPARI

DALIA
CENTRAL
NMATJ
B E D E D O
PINTUBI
JU MU
ARA
(WE

KUKATJA

DA:DADJARA
PIT JANDJARA
AHTAKI

BA
NANA

STRALIA
MANDJINDJA
SO

LKADJARA

NADATADJARA
D'A L E A

WA: LJEN
WONGA:I
KO

GA:
TJERARIDJA:L
MURUNITJA
AUST

M I R N I D
WIR

DADJUNMA
AUSTRALIAN

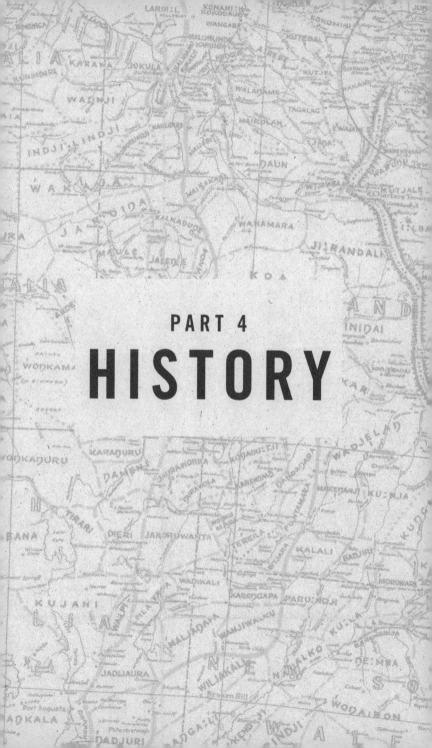

PART 4

HISTORY

BETWEEN DISCOVERY
AND HOPE

The eleventh of June 1770: for Lieutenant James Cook the end looms near. His ship the *Endeavour* has run aground on the Great Barrier Reef. This man of the sea fears he will now be lost to it. Cook sees his men grow desperate; hope is fading. He dreads that in a little time they will turn violently on each other. Those who survive will anyway be dead to the world; what is left of their lives lost in a wilderness. Cook's journal counts every passing hour, his mood ever darker.

> ... death has approached in all his terrors; and as the
> dreadful moment that was to determine our fate came on,
> every one saw his own sensations pictured in the
> countenances of his companions ...

Cook's life, the lives of his crew, hang on the winds and the water. Everything that can be spared is tossed overboard; with the load lighter and the tide rising, the vessel heaves into the deep water. The crew that had slumped exhausted on deck lift their spirits for a final effort. All hands man the pump to hold the incoming flood at bay. It is on these moments history turns. To read Cook's words takes my breath away. Here is a man far from his home, commanding a ship on a voyage to lands whispered of and imagined. Through his words I see him; not a cast-iron figure – a statue – but the man James Cook; a man of doubt and fear and perseverance and undoubted courage.

Cook had navigated the waters of the eastern coast of this southern continent, his maps recording his journey. On 22 August 1770 Lieutenant James Cook claimed the whole of the territory at Pòssession Island. This land would now be known as New South Wales. As an Indigenous person, my admiration for his feats is mixed with the reality that he looked upon my ancestors as, in his words, 'some of the most rude and uncivilised upon the earth'. The events his voyage set in train would prove devastating for my family; its legacy hangs heavily still in Indigenous lives today. Yet, Cook brought also the fruits of the Enlightenment, he brought the science of Sir Isaac Newton, he brought the thoughts of John Locke, the father of liberalism, whose ideas had inspired revolution and democracy. By planting the British flag, Cook also sowed the seeds of British law, and it was that legal system which would ultimately deliver justice for Indigenous Australians. Two centuries after Cook's arrival, Australia's High Court would strike down the lie of terra nullius. In the historic case *Mabo v Queensland (No 2)*, the court recognised the legal claims to land of the First Peoples of Australia. Captain Cook was wrong, this was not an *empty* land, my ancestors were not uncivilised brutes, they had a system of law that gave them title to this land, title that endures today.

James Cook and Eddie Mabo bookend our nation's story, but they hold an even greater place in the history of the world. In

2001 UNESCO compiled what it called the *Memory of the World*, Australia had two entries: the *Journal of Captain James Cook* and the *Personal Papers of Eddie Koiki Mabo*. This is my history, from Cook to Mabo, from *Terra Nullius* to *Native Title*. This is the history of all of us who call Australia home.

*

I was wrong about Captain Cook. In 2017, I reflected on his legacy and statues in his honour as a debate raged around the world about monuments, their meaning and whether they should be torn down. The United States was in the grip of a culture war; statues commemorating Confederate Civil War figures were being toppled. The distinctive Confederate flag, which had been so identified with racism and white supremacy, was being lowered. This culture war reached its bloodiest point in Charlottesville, Virginia on 11 August 2017. Neo-Confederates, neo-fascists, neo-Nazis and nationalists gathered for a rally to 'Unite the Right'. They were motivated by moves to take down a statue of Confederate General Robert E. Lee.

The rally turned violent with clashes erupting against anti-fascist groups. One white supremacist rammed his car into a crowd, killing a young woman. In the end more than thirty people were injured. History was being weaponised; a battle over the past and who had a right to their story had pitched Americans against each other.

At the time I wondered about our different histories, how Americans grapple – uncomfortably, even violently – with their dark past and how in Australia we have preferred silence. In an article for the ABC Online website, I wrote of walking past a

statue of Captain Cook in Sydney's Hyde Park. I had passed by so
many times and barely given it a second thought, but on this day
I stopped and read the inscription. The words told me that Cook
'Discovered This Territory 1770'. I wondered at this word
'discovered'. It was a word from a time when this land was
declared empty, when the rights of the people who had been here
for thousands of generations were extinguished. Discovery was
never just a word, it was a doctrine.

As I wrote in the article, the statue spoke to how differently
we – black and white – see our national story:

> It has stood since 1879. When it was unveiled more than
> 60,000 people turned out. The procession at the time was
> the largest ever seen in Sydney.
>
> No one present then questioned that this was the man
> who founded the nation.
>
> But think about that today. Think of those words:
> 'Discovered this territory.'
>
> My ancestors were here when Cook dropped anchor. We
> know now that the first peoples of this continent had been
> here for at least 65,000 years, for us the beginning of human
> time.
>
> Yet this statue speaks to emptiness, it speaks to our
> invisibility; it says that nothing truly mattered, nothing
> truly counted until a white sailor first walked on these
> shores.
>
> The statue speaks still to terra nullius and the violent
> rupture of Aboriginal society and a legacy of pain and
> suffering that endures today.

The inscription that Cook 'Discovered This Territory 1770' maintained a myth, a belief in the superiority of white Christendom that had historically devastated indigenous peoples everywhere. Where does that myth come from? In 1452 Pope Nicholas V sanctioned the conquest, colonisation and exploitation of all non-Christian peoples. In 1493, after Christopher Columbus returned from his so-called 'discovery' of America, Pope Alexander VI decreed that land not ruled by Christian kings was free to be claimed.

The idea of terra nullius was the law of whiteness, that anyone who did not worship Jesus Christ was less than human. The doctrines of discovery and terra nullius have been demolished by the church, by our courts, by the United Nations. The UN Permanent Forum on Indigenous Issues says the discovery doctrine is the 'foundation of the violation of [Indigenous peoples'] human rights'.

I wondered how in Australia we could maintain the ceremonial fig leaf of welcomes to country while a statue stood in the centre of our largest city proclaiming to the world that no one here mattered until a white person *discovered* the land? It spoke to an enduring problem in Australia, a land of gestures and tokens of respect and recognition, but still with no substantial recognition of Indigenous peoples. There remain no treaties with Indigenous people – the only Commonwealth country without one – and a stubborn political resistance to constitutional reform that would give Indigenous peoples a voice in our founding document that was originally written to exclude them.

As I wrote in my original article, the comparison to the United States was revealing:

Yes, America tears itself apart trying to make itself better.

Race: Americans cannot ignore it, cannot deny it, cannot hide from it.

But what about us?

America cannot avoid the legacy of racism. We find it all too easy to avoid.

If America seeks to find what Lincoln called 'the better angels of our nature', we vanish into the 'Great Australian Silence'.

Anthropologist Bill Stanner coined that phrase in the 1960s to describe what he said was 'a cult of forgetting practised on a national scale'.

We have chosen to ignore our heritage. So much history here remains untold.

My mind goes back to another journey, well before Cook, a journey unrecorded in any logbook. It is written on the landscape, on cave walls; its trail uncovered today in fossilised remains, so ancient is this story. It is the journey of a people completing that epic human trek out of Africa. These people had come as far as the Indonesian archipelago and now eyed another land in the distance: a final home.

Perhaps they saw smoke from wildfires, perhaps they kept moving because that's what people do. Something put them in boats to make what was then the first open sea journey in the history of humanity. Somewhere lost in time the first footprints appeared on this soil. Archaeological evidence now dates human occupation in Australia from at least 65,000 years ago. To the people who would create new cultures here, tell new stories, this time is not time at all; it is The Dreaming. Sixty-five thousand years; it is easy to say but so daunting, so awe-inspiring to contemplate. Two-hundred and forty-nine years of British possession; 65,000 years of the First People.

I thought about those things as I watched the spectre of American history cast a dark shadow over that nation. I pondered the questions of heritage and hate. Statues were coming down, old flags of division were being put away and a country was tearing itself apart. Fascists, neo-Nazis and Klansmen who wrapped themselves in the flag of the Confederacy were reigniting the old grievances of the Civil War. How did a nation reckon with itself? What was the balance of history? Could it be weighed and measured? Is it possible to ever truly atone for our past? Abraham Lincoln's Emancipation Proclamation – freeing the slaves – Martin Luther King's dream, the Civil Rights marches that brought an end to segregation, the election of the first black president, Barack Obama, none of these things truly healed America's wound.

Across Australia there are monuments to settlers and explorers, those who drove Aboriginal people from their lands. Where though are the markers of our frontier battles? There is still no place on the Australian War Memorial Roll of Honour for those Aboriginal people who died on this soil fighting to defend their country. This is what Indigenous people mean when we talk about 'truth telling', a full account of our history that doesn't diminish the suffering or the humanity of the First Peoples. History is so quickly captured by the culture warriors, turned into a political battle of left versus right. The German philosopher Karl Lowith once wrote: 'To ask earnestly the question of the ultimate meaning of history takes one's breath away.' As the lessons of the United States teach us, history is perilous territory; history can so easily inflame old hatreds.

That's what I got so wrong about Captain Cook. I had forgotten the words of the great African-American emancipation fighter and philosopher Frederick Douglass, who said, 'we have to do with the past only as we can make it useful to the present and the future'. I was not wrong to ask questions about the idea of discovery. I was not wrong to ask why we in Australia too easily turn away from history we don't like. But did I feed a narrative of grievance? Did I turn Australian history into a battleground? Is it even possible to debate history without first loading our guns?

Within weeks of my article on Captain Cook the history warriors were out in force. I was public enemy number one, accused of inciting hatred. Those who hold the pen of Australian history refused to give up, they had written the final chapter and shut the book. To them I was committing a heresy; it was treasonous. Prime Minister Malcolm Turnbull lectured us that history cannot be rewritten. The more excitable media carried headlines of 'Stalinism', *Taliban Stan* some called me, as though my challenge to the myth of discovery was akin to terrorists tearing down the Buddhas of Bamiyan.

But there were two sides to this culture war; on the other were those who viewed Captain Cook as a symbol of entrenched racism in Australia. They wanted the statue torn down. It was the last thing I wanted; I made that clear. I had argued explicitly that the monument remain intact, but that we revise the plaque or add an inscription recognising the place of Indigenous people. I had tried to find a middle ground, where none existed. I had disturbed the ghosts of our past. I felt my world turning on its axis; when debate turns to hysteria no one listens. It was all I could do to batten down and wait for the storm to pass; but within days it flared again.

I was at my son's basketball game when I heard the news that someone had sprayed the Cook statue with graffiti. It made me feel ill; at some level I had to own that, I had to accept that the words I set loose in the world had led to this. This wasn't about the past, it was about now; this was history as identity.

How can we hope to be honest about our past when we use history as a weapon to bludgeon each other? When it comes to history we pick our sides and we tell our stories and the space between us grows. Statues and monuments tell us who we are; they tell us what we choose to forget and what we remember and there is no more powerful symbol of Australia than Captain Cook and terra nullius. The Cook statue tells us everything about us; triumph and discovery, and absence, loss and emptiness. Martin Luther King Jnr was so right, 'we are not makers of history, we are made by history'.

The beauty of writing, for me, is that it allows me to express how I feel right now; to put down my thoughts, to argue my case. Writing is a clearing house for ideas; once written down there is space to think new thoughts. In writing I wrestle with my country, I struggle with myself. If I were to write that article today, it would be different. I would still question the doctrine of discovery; I would still argue that we cannot simply bury our past. But my mistake was to buy into the idea that the arrival of Cook sealed the fate of my ancestors. Yes, it altered the course of our history, but *history* did not end. History is not a balance sheet where we tally victories and defeats. History is not events, dates, places or names. History – if it is to make any sense to me – is a story of us and how we meet each other.

I return to the words of Cook, stricken on the Great Barrier Reef. The place where he had first struck peril he called Cape

Tribulation. He had feared the worst, yet had come through, and he passed two small islands which at the height of his distress he had resigned himself to never reaching. In his journal he wrote:

> They had been the object of our hope, or perhaps rather our wishes, and therefore I called them HOPE ISLANDS.

As Cook patched up his stricken *Endeavour* he spent more than a month on the land of the Guugu Yimithirr. Here one of the crew saw an odd-looking animal, something he had never seen before. He motioned to one of the local people, asking what it was. 'Ganguru' was the reply. He wrote it down as 'Kangaroo'. A new word had entered English; no longer a Guugu Yimithirr word, not quite an English word. Now, it was a distinctively Australian word: a new language born on this soil.

THE OWL OF MINERVA

I was eighteen when I arrived at the University of New South Wales in Sydney. It was a world for which I was utterly unprepared. No one in my family had ever completed high school, university was not even spoken of. There were a handful of other Aboriginal students, and we clung to each other. I was so intimidated I barely left my room in the college dorm. I would wait until the other students had gone to the dining hall and then sneak out under darkness to eat at some local take away. My university life began as Australia was waking up to its past; the Great Australian Silence was being pierced by a new generation of historians. Henry Reynolds wrote of life on the other side of the frontier, he wrote of massacres and war. Lyndall Ryan reminded us of the attempt to exterminate the First Peoples of Tasmania. It was a story I had grown up with, a people extinct, wiped out with the death of the 'Last Tasmanian', Truganini. What happened, I was taught, on that remote island stood as condemnation of the brutality of the British but it also reinforced the story of the doomed fate of Aboriginal people; that we were a people who faded from the landscape. Lyndall Ryan turned that on its head: the people had not died out but lived on in their descendants, the offspring of Aboriginal women and white sailors and whalers. This was a thriving distinct community – just like my own – but one living under the burden of the myth of extinction. A race of people to be pitied but unseen.

These were vital corrections to a whitewashed history that had blanked out the worst of the frontier. For me, though, this revisionist history was something more. It took on the importance of myth, it gave me a story to live by. As Australians we turn to the Anzac legend and the courage of Kokoda as evidence of Aussie fighting spirit; I looked to the massacres, the poisoned flour, the miserable missions, to revel in Australia's shame. These stories, I thought, explained my world: we were the victimised, trampled on as the real Australians built this nation. Historians have called this 'the invention of tradition'; if I believed we had lost our place in the world, I could recreate a glorious struggle against a vicious enemy. Soon I began to act it out, I wore land rights T-shirts and took to tying my hair in a black, red and yellow headband, the colours of the Aboriginal flag. A year earlier I had been going to pubs, watching rock bands with my mostly white mates, wearing a mod jacket festooned with a Union Jack and emblazoned with the name The Jam, my favourite English rockers. I had gone from little Englander to budding black activist – from Michael Caine to Malcolm X – in a matter of months.

It was the German philosopher Hegel who once wrote, 'the owl of Minerva spreads its wings only with the falling of dusk'. What Hegel meant was that we only truly see history as it passes; wisdom is gained only in hindsight.

Reading Hegel is an exhilarating experience, although it can be hard going; his writing swings from impenetrable and abstruse, to sublime. His ideas have as much as any philosopher helped shape our modern world. Along with Immanuel Kant and Friedrich Nietzsche, Hegel has been the thinker I have returned to time and again to shine a light into the darkest corners. They're like code breakers, making sense of the otherwise indecipherable noise of humanity. Their ideas can be truly terrifying, like a rip in the ocean that drags the swimmer beyond the breakers and into the deep water; the only way back to shore is to stay afloat. Each has been linked to some of the worst of humanity: Hegel to the rise of Nazism, communism and totalitarianism; Nietzsche likewise and appropriated today by the resurgent alt-right nationalists; and Kant linked by some to racist imperialism. Yet despite that, they are indispensable; their ideas greater than those who have appropriated them.

Think of what they ask of us. Kant and his ideas of universal humanity, a cosmopolitanism that shatters allegiance to fixed identities: nation, race or faith; Hegel and his belief that freedom is only attainable through the ultimate spirit and that spirit resides in the state; and Nietzsche with his warning that we have killed God, and elevated the individual to the point where we are devoid of meaning, a rootless species believing in nothing, 'men without chests'.

Reading philosophy, great thinkers like John Locke, David Hume and John Stuart Mill, is the reason that I recoil from the latter-day denunciation of the Western tradition; those who dismiss these figures as merely 'dead white men'. These thinkers laid the platform for liberalism, democracy, human rights, globalisation, and yes, patriarchy, white privilege, structural inequality. This is our world, this is what we wrestle with and this is why I return again and again to these giant figures of intellectual history.

For me it is Hegel who opens a window onto understanding the forces of history. His is a philosophy of history that looks beyond the catalogue of events – the great figures, the wars and disasters, the rise and fall of empires – to a quest, a human quest to live another day, to search for meaning, to seek new ways to live together, to confront our worst and ask what it is to be human. Hegel saw his task as writing history as philosophy; it was the grandest undertaking of all, not a history of a people or a nation, but what he called a 'Universal History'. Read what he wrote in his famous lecture on history:

> It is not history itself that is here presented. We might more properly designate it as a History of History; a criticism of historical narratives and an investigation of their truth and credibility.

Hegel said that we are rational beings, and that reason 'is the sovereign of the world'; therefore history must be a 'rational process'. To explain history, wrote Hegel, is to 'depict the passions of mankind', to observe the 'great stage' and divine 'the plan of providence'. History was progress, and progress was the road to freedom. Hegel charted a geographical course through the span of humanity from, he said, Eastern nations who 'knew only that one is free', to the Greek and Roman worlds where 'only some are free', to a point in the future – an absolute spirit, a zeitgeist – where 'all men absolutely (man as man) are free'. Hegel sought clarity in a world of seemingly brutal chaos; history, he said, can be a 'slaughter-bench at which the happiness of people, the wisdom of States, and the virtue of individuals have been victimised'. The task, he said, was to find the principle, the final aim of 'these enormous sacrifices'. History he said, was 'not the theatre of happiness', happiness is a 'blank page' in history; history is driven by disruption; it is the emergence of an antithesis that forces change. To Hegel, history was the human quest for freedom and recognition.

Hegel has been many things to many people; there are Hegelians on the political right and left. Karl Marx drew on Hegel's philosophy of history for his own work *Das Kapital*, especially seizing on the inherent contradictions – the thesis-antithesis – that Hegel believed was the engine of change. For Marx that was captured in the struggle between the workers and the bosses, the Proletariat and the Bourgeoisie. Marx was inspired by Hegel but he also sought to turn the philosopher on his head; where Hegel saw 'absolute spirit' culminating in the state, Marx saw the state upended by the workers' revolution.

In our time, the American political scientist, Francis Fukuyama, drew on Hegel for his famous 'End of History' thesis. In 1989, Fukuyama seized on the end of the Cold War to declare that the great ideological battles had been fought and won. Fukuyama, then a little-known analyst at the US State Department, penned an essay for the magazine *National Interest*, in which he argued that we were seeing the triumph of the West, that liberal democracy may constitute the 'end point of mankind's ideological evolution – the final form of human government': indeed the end of history.

It may sound strange: 'the end of history'. Of course history does not end, there are always events and twists and turns in the fortunes of human beings, but Fukuyama was talking about history in a different and altogether more profound sense. He was talking about history as the struggle for justice, for freedom and for recognition; he was talking about an arc of progress that he believed had now delivered humanity to its summit. This was Hegel's idea of the absolute spirit. It was Hegel who first believed he had seen the 'end of history', when he glimpsed the triumphant Napoleon after the Battle of Jena in 1806, saying: 'I saw the emperor – this world-spirit – go out from the city to survey his realm ... stretching over the world and dominating it.' History did not end, not in Napoleon's time and certainly not at the end of the Cold War, and there is a potential for Hegel's ideas to lead to triumphalism, yet there is something still so tantalising for me about humanity's quest for freedom.

How does Hegel speak to history in my country? Freedom, recognition? As the world was subject to revolution and upheaval, so the arrival of the British was a rupture in the lives of the people whose civilisation had endured here largely untouched for thousands of years. It did indeed represent a 'slaughter-bench', but what was the 'plan of providence'? Following Hegel's arc of history, if Indigenous society was the thesis, the arrival of Captain Cook was the antithesis; the centrifugal force that tilted the axis of life here, am I and people like me not it's synthesis? I am born of black and white, formed out of a collision of such vastly different cultures. Critics of this Hegelian idea of a history of progress see fatalism; that the destination exists ahead of the journey. There is also an inherent ethnocentrism; a belief in the triumph of the West. It is true that Hegel saw history through a European lens, freedom like the sun dawned in the east and set in the west. As Hegelian scholar Terry Pinkard writes on Hegel, 'European modernity is where things had ended up. And the foreseeable future was, so he thought, ineluctably going to be a version of European modernity.'

It is inarguable that the revolutions – technological, industrial, philosophical – begun in eighteenth-century Europe have transformed our world. Democracy, capitalism, freedom of expression, universal rights, individualism, rule of law, separation of church and state, accelerated change in a way never before seen in human history. We are today more literate, more materially wealthy, and healthier than ever before. We are more connected to each other, borders have come down and trade moves more freely. Peoples have thrown off the yoke of imperialism and have looked to bodies forged out of Enlightenment principles of liberalism, like the United Nations, to enshrine the rights of previously colonised or indigenous peoples. As I will write later, liberalism has sown the seeds of both destruction and liberation.

In Ancient Greece, Hegel saw the birth of a polis, a democracy, where citizens could be bound together and pursue their ambitions and desires. As Hegel called it, the birth of a 'beautiful individuality'. Yet everything holds its own contradiction. As Athens celebrated the rights of citizens it barred others from joining that citizenship, and Greece could not have existed without slavery. In our time, we too struggle with the realities of democracy and market economy that contain their own exclusion and inequality. But to Hegel, those contradictions, that tension, is essential, the very locus of change. There are some who see the arrival of the British on this land as an end: a cataclysm. But is it not also a beginning? The civilisation that existed here had been remarkable for its ability to thrive in a hot, dry, isolated continent. It had an intricate social structure, kinship laws and ceremony that gave people a deep belonging and connection to place and each other. The Dreaming met the Enlightenment, and people met each other. We cannot pretend it was an equal exchange; disease and violence tore through the local populations, but history – Hegel's philosophy of history – was doing its work.

We are all set on a journey that Hegel believed gave us our best hope of liberation. We look to others for recognition as they look to be recognised by us. For much of my life I have seen history as a ball and chain, something from which it was impossible to be untethered; something at best to be endured. Hegel's ideas of becoming – change, driven by rupture – has helped ease the burden. We are not locked in time and place, we are on a journey. Yet history haunts us, it whispers in our ears, voices of our ancestors, from old wars, pitting us still against each other.

TO REMEMBER TO FORGET

You know that old saying of George Santayana, 'those who do not remember the past are condemned to repeat it'? It's a moral lesson meant to save us from ourselves. But what if we cling too tightly to the past? History is a weapon; it is to identity what carbon is to steel. From history we construct our own self-image, and it is the history of grievance that seems to have the deadliest hold. In three decades of reporting around the world, I have seen how history and memory are the breath that reignites the still-smouldering embers of hatred. Think of the conflicts of our time – Hutu versus Tutsi in Rwanda, Catholic against Protestant in Northern Ireland, the blood feuds between Sunni and Shi'a Islam, Hindu and Muslim – the nuclear-armed tension between North and South Korea. In every case they are tied to identities forged in the fire of age-old battles.

The Indian philosopher and economist Amartya Sen has written extensively about issues of identity and justice. He warns of what he calls 'solitarist identities': the dangers of limited or restrictive ideas of identity. A solitarist approach, he says, can be a good way of misunderstanding nearly everyone in the world. As he wrote, 'Identity can also kill – and kill with abandon.'

History is the pulse of the populist politics of identity; history as betrayal; a narrative of loss, of inheritance robbed. This history looms over the present, obscuring progress; there is just the past framing the present and denying the future. In his 2017 book *In Praise of Forgetting*, journalist and philosopher David Rieff challenged the idea of memory, history and identity. Rieff warned 'thinking about history is far more likely to paralyse than encourage'. He says we risk turning it into a 'formula for unending grievance and vendetta'.

Rieff's book is small but powerful. It was published at a time when I was confronting these questions in my own life. Was my identity tied to memory? Did I see myself as a reflection of a history of loss? I was not alone in linking history to justice; as the Jewish writer, activist and Nobel Laureate Elie Wiesel said, 'Justice without memory is incomplete'. But what was memory anyway? How reliable could it be? We talk about collective memory, as though we experience history equally and together. Yet memory, we know, is personal and fallible. History handed down through story changes with the telling. I learned my history at the feet of my parents, listening to the stories of their lives and the lives of their parents and grandparents. These memories became as real as my own; their pain became my pain.

Historian Jacques Le Goff wrote, 'Memory only seeks to rescue the past in order to serve the present and future.' He is telling us that memory is selective, we choose our stories to give us a *sense* of the past, but it will always be incomplete. We view history backwards always from the vantage point of today as if it holds the secrets to who and what we are. As an Aboriginal boy feeling marginalised and stigmatised my parents' stories of injustice and suffering helped explain what put us here; Australia was to blame. But memory is not history; as David Rieff said, 'The takeover of history by memory is also the takeover of history by politics.' My identity was deeply political; something shaped in opposition to Australia. It was an identity of defiance; I railed against the white blood in me. Memory is not only selective, it is unimpeachable, it is intimate, passed down through the generations, an inheritance from parents to children. To question this was to question family: it was betrayal. Memory is a chain linking us to a past from which we forge our identity. At its best it has given me a place to belong and a pride in my heritage and my family's resilience. But there is a downside. Bitter memory can poison the soul; at its worst it can feel more like a noose, strangling us, choking us off from the world.

Memory is the foundation of what has been called the *invention of tradition.* People the world over do this, blending history and politics into culture and identity. The Irish Grants – the white descendants of convict John Grant – are still said to sing rebel songs at family reunions. The Irish are not dissimilar to Indigenous Australians, indeed people like me of Irish and Aboriginal heritage are sometimes referred to as *shamrock Aborigines.* David Rieff wrote his book *In Praise of Forgetting* while living in Dublin. He says, 'the mythical Ireland still to be found in the frozen republicanism of a declining portion of the Irish diaspora'. As I was raised on the stories of the oppression of my black forebears, generations of Irish have been raised on the story of the persecution of Catholics, the pillage of Oliver Cromwell. Rieff quotes Irish historian John M. Regan, who saw this foundation myth as 'the immemorial struggle against English misrule ... eulogised physical force and honoured the pieties of separatist republican-nationalism'.

In the 1970s a new generation of Aboriginal activists embraced a burgeoning black nationalism. As a boy entering his teens, I was captivated by this radicalism: the Tent Embassy and Land Rights marches. I read about Black Power, black nationalist movements of the United States. It was a political awakening for me, I can see now I was naive and misguided but I have a lingering affection for that youthful me; he was curious, willing to think new thoughts. I see my younger self in the righteous anger of Indigenous protesters today, burning Australian flags and denouncing Australia Day. Perhaps there was a time I might have been among them, but years as a reporter, wading through bloodshed, seeing how historical grievance can pit people against each other, how history filtered through memory can distort our view of the world, I am more inclined to the suggestion of Irish literary critic Edna Longley: perhaps we should raise a monument to amnesia, and forget where we put it.

*

French philosopher and writer Albert Camus said, 'All revolutionaries finally aspire to world unity and act as though they believed that history were dead.' The story of modern times is humanity's struggle with history. History has been buried so many times ... and history always returns. In fact, when it comes to history, I am reminded of the words of the playwright Eugene O'Neill, who wrote, 'There is no present or future – only the past, happening over and over again – now.'

When I look at our world today I wonder, are we locked in some never-ending cycle – a death spiral from which we cannot pull out? The embers of old wars are flaring again: North Korea has enough nuclear weapons to turn our region into a sea of fire. It has the missile capability to deliver its payload as far away as the United States or Australia. The world's two biggest nuclear-armed states, Russia and the United States, are threatening a new Cold War. In 2017, old foes India and China – the most populous nations on the planet – eyeballed each other over disputed territory on their borders. Troops on both sides readied for battle; we came so close to a war with unthinkable consequences.

In the Middle East the Syrian conflict rages on. Refugee camps are full. People are risking all to pile onto boats and hope to reach safety on whatever far shore will take them.

In Yemen the two biggest powers in the Muslim world, Iran and Saudi Arabia, are locked in a deadly proxy war – pitting Shi'a Houthi rebels backed by Tehran against the Yemeni government. As many as 85,000 children under the age of five are thought to have starved to death in Yemen in the past three years. Take a look at the images of the emaciated children, eyes bulging, loose skin, exposed rib cages – precisely the sort of images we saw out of Ethiopia in the 1980s, when the world's music stars rallied in aid concerts and records, and governments stepped up and we all swore never again. But as I write, Yemen is facing the greatest humanitarian disaster of the twenty-first century – 14 million people are at risk and it is all so preventable, if only the Saudis would lift their blockade of the border that is strangling civilian access to food, fuel and desperately needed aid.

A war on terrorism that began – officially at least – after the attack on the United States on 11 September 2001, rages on. It is the longest war America has fought; it is the longest war in Australia's history. Nowhere is safe. Terrorists have struck in London, Brussels, Nairobi, Jakarta, Sydney and Melbourne.

Russia stares down Ukraine. Pakistan and India remain locked in a nuclear-armed existential stand-off. All of this, happening during what is considered to be the longest period of global peace in human history. It hardly feels like it.

But there is an even greater fear: a war between the two biggest powers on the globe, the United States and China. The battle plans are already being drawn up. Any clash between the US and China is potentially catastrophic, but as much as we may try to wish it away, right now military strategists in Beijing and Washington are preparing for just such an eventuality. In 2015 global think-tank the Rand Corporation prepared a report for the American military. Its title could not have been more direct: *War with China: Thinking Through the Unthinkable*. It concluded that China would suffer greater casualties than the US if war was to break out now. However, it cautioned that as China's military muscle increased so would the prospect of a prolonged destructive war.

This is the world I have reported on. In thirty years of journalism the theme I have returned to again and again is history: the role it plays in our lives; how tightly we cling to it; how it defines us; how easy it is to twist and bend the story of the past into an unending narrative of resentment. History is the weapon of choice of authoritarians and demagogues. Everywhere there is resurgent populism, nationalism, sectarianism, tribalism. All of it feeds on history.

I see these same forces playing out in my own country, among people I would call my own. The narrative of historical loss, of humiliation, has helped shape my sense of myself as it has for other Indigenous people. As the Chinese remember their humiliation by foreign powers, as Russians lament the end of the Soviet empire, as Shi'a and Sunni Muslims set themselves against each other in a conflict rooted in the past, so memory defines identity; it cannot be divorced from history. It is what Czeslaw Milosz called 'the memory of wounds'.

*

'I just want to know how to sleep at night.'

The old man had come in from the bush to Alice Springs for a suicide prevention conference I was due to speak at. He had lost a nephew and a grandson to suicide. Like so many Indigenous people across this country he was mourning another lost generation. He was not alone. Brothers, sisters, sons and daughters had all gone before their time. This is a story so common to Indigenous families it links us in a shared sadness that stretches across the centuries.

'I just want to know how to sleep at night.'

The old man wasn't speaking just of suicide; he spoke to the sleeplessness of a people who are struggling to hold themselves against the world; to keep out the memories of wounds.

The memory of wounds, Indigenous people know are their memories. These are the memories far too many are born into. Memories of loss and sadness; memories of grief. This is an inheritance of grief. These memories are not just carried within; these memories seep deep into the soil. The very land itself can feel heavy with despair – the rolling hills, the jagged mountains, the deserts and plains – all of it can feel so terribly sad. I have felt it on those times when I am sitting alone or driving. I have felt it sitting beside our waterholes and rivers.

The memory of wounds. For some Indigenous people, pain is how they recognise themselves. For some – for me at times – it has been easier to live in sadness than to embrace joy. Sadness is so familiar that happiness can be suspect; sadness has come to tell us who we are. It is the well from which we draw our identities. Happiness can feel like surrender, like letting go of the memory of wounds – memories that keep our families, our past alive.

It is something common to people living with a traumatic history the world over. The Jewish-American writer Elizabeth Rosner has reckoned with the memory of wounds in her book *Survivor Café*. Her parents were Holocaust survivors and her identity was framed around a legacy of pain. As she wrote, 'I am more afraid of forgetting my parents' stories than I am of forgetting my own.' Elizabeth Rosner says we are all 'trapped in our nightmares'.

I have spoken and written about my own family's history; our own nightmares. In 2016, after publishing *Talking to My Country*, I was invited to speak at the National Press Club and chose as my theme 'The Weight of History'.

In the 1940s a man named Budyaan spoke this same language to his grandson in the main street of his hometown. Police overheard him, he was arrested and taken to jail. Budyaan, was also known as Wilfred Johnson, my great-grandfather. The boy he spoke to that day was my father, Stan Grant senior. Budyaan and his grandson were living under the weight of our history.

In 1894, Lydia Naden was a frightened young girl, living on a mission called Warangesda, at Darlington Point on the banks of the Murrumbidgee River. Lydia was hiding out in one of the mission huts. Girls were being rounded up and

forced into a dormitory where they would be separated from
their families and trained to become domestic servants.
Lydia's resistance was in vain, she was discovered, taken to
the dormitory where she not only lost her liberty but was
starved as a punishment. The mission records show her food
ration was cut.

Lydia Naden was living with the weight of history.

Lydia eventually married a man named Frank Foster,
who as a boy in the 1880s was snatched from his birthplace
in Sydney and taken to the newly created Aboriginal
mission at Maloga on the Murray River. In turn he was
sent to Warangesda until he was banished for being
insolent and impudent, for daring to challenge authority.
He spent his days wandering the state looking for a home,
turning up in reports from the Protector of Aborigines
until his death in 1940. Lydia Naden and Frank Foster had
a daughter, who in turn would have a daughter of her own,
who she named Josie. She became my paternal
grandmother: born into the burden of the weight of our
history.

I have a photograph of a group of Aboriginal girls
standing in line outside the notorious welfare home in
Cootamundra. None of them are smiling and I am drawn
to the eyes of one young girl, staring blankly ahead. She is
known by a number: number 658. This girl – number
658 – was recommended for removal from her family by
the manager of the Aboriginal station at Cowra. Number
658 was just one of so many of what have been called 'the
Stolen Generations': children separated from their loved
ones.

Many were forever lost, never to find their way back home. Number 658 was eventually sent to work as a maid for wealthy squatter families. Her life was controlled by the state. She had to seek approval and permission to marry the man she loved and eventually to live on an Aboriginal mission at Condobolin in western New South Wales, alongside her long-lost brother. Number 658 would die a young woman, only thirty-seven years old, from rheumatic fever she first contracted in the girls home. She left behind six young orphaned children: lives weighed down by our history. Number 658 had a name; a name taken from her, Eunice Josephine Grant. She was my great-aunt, the sister of my grandfather.

I am the sum of these lives. The stories of Budyaan, Lydia, Frank and Eunice inform who I am as surely as their blood courses through my veins. This is part of my inheritance: I bear the burden and pride and the responsibility of the weight of this history.

For a people shaped by the darkest forces of our world, forgetting can be a troubling idea. It can feel like betrayal. Here is the big test of forgetting: are we prepared to sacrifice justice for peace? Think about that: we can pursue justice, we can litigate the past in an endless Nuremberg trial, or we can choose peace and put the bones of our ancestors to rest and know that their struggle and their suffering released us from their burden; delivered us a new day.

That was the choice facing South Africa at the end of Apartheid. Justice or peace – it was that simple. They could pursue the crimes of apartheid and prosecute the perpetrators or they could let truth set them free. Listen again to the words of Desmond Tutu: forgiveness and reconciliation are the 'only truly viable alternatives to revenge, retribution and reprisal'.

'Without forgiveness' – he said – 'there is no future.'

Archbishop Tutu headed a 'truth and reconciliation commission' not a 'truth and justice commission'. Justice perhaps would have been easier and it would have electrified the blood of a people with every cause for vengeance. By choosing peace, Tutu set South African people a more Godly task:

> Forgiveness is not facile or cheap. It is a costly business that makes those who are willing to forgive even more extraordinary.

Forgetting is essential for forgiveness, we cannot truly forgive while we hold onto the wrong; but forgetting is not 'getting over it'. How often do we hear that: Why can't you move on? That is the demand of the politician who thinks sorry is enough; who grows impatient when the victims do not fully embrace their former tormentors. That is politics. Forgetting is not political; it is something stronger than politics: it is love.

I spent enough time as a boy in the black church of the Aboriginal mission of my childhood, where we would return time and again – enough hours fidgeting and wishing I was swimming in the river – enough time listening to my uncle, the spit and thunder, fire and brimstone preacher – to remember the lesson of *Corinthians* in the rolling cadence of the King James Bible:

> And now abideth faith, hope, charity, these three: but the greatest of these three is charity.

You don't have to be a believer – to accept all the orthodoxy of the church – to be in awe of the Jesus on the cross who disavows vengeance:

Father forgive them for they know not what they do.

*

But are there crimes so monstrous they cannot be forgiven – are their sins so heinous that they cannot be moved from history to mere memory? The Austrian philosopher Jean Amery refused to let go of the horrors of the Holocaust ... he refused to forget what he had seen. He railed against what he called 'the hollow, thoughtless, utterly false conciliatoriness or the pathos of forgiveness and reconciliation'. His anger was as righteous as Desmond Tutu's love. Amery's words are chilling:

What happened, happened. But that it happened cannot be so easily accepted. I rebel: against my past, against history, and against a present that places the incomprehensible in the cold storage of history.

Jean Amery was born as Hans Meier in 1912 – his father Jewish but his mother Catholic. Under new laws passed in 1935, he became legally recognised as Jewish and that would in time become a death sentence. In 1938 he fled to Belgium but by 1943 he was caught and tortured by the Gestapo. He was eventually sent to Auschwitz. He arrived with 655 others – 417 of whom were immediately killed. He saw the brutality of the Nazis, how they imposed their views of Aryan supremacy, and wrote that 'the world always dies where the claim of some reality is total'.

Jean Amery never relinquished his resentment – he thought it a betrayal. For him there would be no place for war monuments acknowledging the Nazi shame or the Jewish suffering – 'to be a victim alone is not an honour', he said. You can read his words in his extraordinary book *Beyond Guilt and Atonement*. I hear Amery and I admit that as someone whose people have suffered in Australia, it touches me profoundly. But in the end I listen to others – to Desmond Tutu – to those lessons in that old black church of my childhood.

And I read the words of Albert Camus: 'Resentment is always resentment against oneself'; resentment turns inward until vengeance destroys us.

Jean Amery who was Hans Meier survived the Nazi death camps – refused to relent in his burning resentment – took his own life at the age of sixty-six in a hotel room in Salzburg.

Jean Amery is Friedrich Nietzsche's '*Ressentiment* Man'. He is a prisoner of his past, defined by historical grievance and driven by hatred and desire for revenge. Where Hegel saw history as progress, the quest for recognition and freedom, '*Ressentiment* Man' is caught in a time warp, returning always to the source of injustice that he cannot fix and does not want to fix. History, for him, is a festering wound, to be picked at over and over, never allowed to heal. His suffering is his strength; his weakness the greatest weapon he has over his oppressor. Nietzsche saw this as the morality of the slave, an inversion of power where the downtrodden emerge triumphant. But to Nietzsche '*Ressentiment* Man' is a loathsome character.

His soul squints; his mind loves hidden crannies, tortuous
paths and backdoors, everything secret appeals to him as
his world, his safety, his balm; he is past master in silence, in
not forgetting ...

'*Ressentiment* Man' plays the psychology of blame; he is a
'whisperer' and 'counterfeiter', whose misery is a favour or a
blessing, something that will one day be compensated.
Forgiveness is the highest virtue and without it there can be no
reconciliation but can we really expect time to heal all wounds?
Are the angry protesters on Australia Day not right to hold
Australia to account?

These are the questions philosopher Thomas Brudholm,
explores in his book *Resentment's Virtue*. He challenges what he
calls the 'boosters of reconciliation', arguing it may be more
moral to refuse to forgive. He confronts Archbishop Tutu, who,
he writes, nowhere 'seriously discusses the possibility that the
preservation of resentment or refusing to forgive might be
justifiable on moral grounds'. He says the Truth and
Reconciliation Commission put a premium on forgiveness when
it 'ought to have been obliged to acknowledge the legitimacy of
anger and the demands for redistributive justice'. Brudholm sees
strength in '*Ressentiment* Man', where Nietzsche saw weakness
and vanity.

In Australia we too wrestle with how to forgive. As
Australians we have marched together for reconciliation, we have
cried together at the national apology to the Stolen Generations,
businesses and government bodies enact reconciliation plans.
There is a simple message: forgiveness is the path to healing.
Reconciliation has been elevated to a national project, with the

risk of its own deadline, a rush to expect Indigenous people to 'move on'. As Brudholm admits:

> Communities can lose patience with survivors and relatives
> who seem stuck in grievances or who appear to nurse their
> victimhood (perhaps for political reasons). At some point,
> societies can tire of survivors' talk of the past and demands
> on the present.

I could never truly let go of the pain of the past, but I can forget and there is a difference: forgetting is not amnesia it is a choice to acknowledge, commemorate and put aside. Ultimately I cannot – will not – give my life to *ressentiment*. Brudholm's argument locks us into an endless cycle of grievance from which there is no escape: it can lead to an early death. Like so many Indigenous people I have felt the push and pull of *ressentiment* and reconciliation; the descendants of the first peoples of Australia have had the farthest distance to travel and the heaviest load to carry on the road to reconciliation. If I look to my family, if I look to the best of Australia, I have to believe in hope, even if that journey can be a wearisome one.

NOSTALGIA FOR
INJUSTICE

I have a very comfortable place in Australia, by any measure mine is a privileged life. If anyone can speak to the possibilities of our country it is me. It is undeniable that Australia has made great progress, Aboriginal people once excluded from this country are now often celebrated. As Maria Lane's study of Aboriginal economic migration showed, there are pathways to success and I am part of this new Indigenous middle class, exploring new ways to be Aboriginal. Yet, there are those moments when all of my success seems meaningless; when the reality of life for too many Aboriginal people shatters the belief in the 'lucky country'.

I remember stepping out into the warm winter sun of a Sydney morning. I wanted to drink in that moment when the sun's rays touch my skin and banish the melancholy I am often prone to carrying inside. It usually works, basking for just a few moments can bring clarity and hope. Not on that day; not even nature's most precious gifts could dispel the gloom I felt about our country.

I could call this anger. I could tell of rage. I could describe a suffocating, nauseating hopelessness. I felt all of that, my mood swung between despair and resignation. Mostly though I just felt sad. The images of boys on my television screen – tear-gassed, beaten, held down, locked up, hooded; boys that look like my boys made me feel foolish, inadequate, for believing in the best of Australia.

I didn't want to watch the 2016 *Four Corners* program on abuse at the Northern Territory Don Dale Youth Detention Centre. I knew what was to come. I couldn't watch all of it. I got up, I walked around and every time I came back there was another boy talking about loneliness and depression and fear. Things once seen cannot be unseen. I carry the twisted images of a lifetime of reporting – bodies broken and lifeless, people screaming in pain, rivers of blood and burning flesh. These are things burned into my eyes and now there is that image of a boy – an Australian boy – bound to a chair, hooded and catatonic.

For Indigenous people these are far too often the images that define Australia.

The next evening I was to give a public lecture at my alma mater, the University of New South Wales. I was receiving a Doctor of Letters, an incredibly proud moment for me and my family. My wife and children were attending and I had worked on a speech that would speak about my hopes for reconciliation. But I was in no mood to put aside old grievances.

*

27 July 2016: University of New South Wales, Sydney

There was a speech I had planned to give tonight. I wished it to be a speech rational and measured.

In this speech I would have appealed to the best of Australia – to what Abraham Lincoln would have called the better angels of our nature.

In this speech I would have wished to locate Indigenous people within the framework of the grand tradition of liberal Western democracy.

In this speech I would have spoken of Hegel's idea of man 'not being at home in the world'. I would have asked how we – the First Peoples of this land – could be at home in a world imposed upon us.

In this speech I would have spoken of Edmund Burke – the father of conservatism – and his template for society: that it be a covenant between those living, those who have passed and those yet to come. What is this covenant that would link my ancestors and my children? For us it would not be the glory of nations won but of nations lost. How then after having our world upended could I pledge allegiance to what has supplanted us?

In this speech I could have touched on those thinkers who are the pillars of Western democratic ideas. I would have told of wrestling with John Locke and J.S. Mill. How they have inspired me yet left me reeling from their implicit harsh judgment of the society and culture that I am drawn from.

I would have told of feeling both drawn to the steadfastness and stoicism of conservatism yet wonder how so many of those who lay claim to the mantle conservative today can be so mean spirited and have a deficit of generosity.

This speech would have looked to contemporary thinkers like Australian Duncan Ivison. Ivison strives for a theory of justice that enables us to feel at home in the world when we are no longer alienated from the institutions and practices of this society, that being at home in the world is not just having to be resigned to accepting or accommodating injustice.

I would have quoted the late American philosopher John Rawls and his idea of reconciliation through public reason; of people being able to endorse the institutions and practices of society and not merely tolerate them. I would have explored what American political scientist William Connolly has termed the 'vital centre of the nation'. I would have returned to John Stuart Mill – the Mill who could speak of a centre that could 'soften the extreme form and fill up the intervals between us'.

This speech I wished to give would have sought amity with a tradition that has excluded us. In this speech I would have sought those things that can unite us not those things that divide. In this speech I would have chosen carefully my words. In this speech I would have sought less to inflame and more to comfort.

I cannot give that speech; it is best saved for another day.

That speech would have come from my head but I wish to speak from my heart.

Some of my own people have criticised me for being too faithful to diplomacy. They find fault in my hope or optimism. To my critics, I give Australia too much credit.

In any other week I might challenge them, but not this week. This week it seems they are right. This week I have struggled to contain a pulsating rage.

I have moved from boiling anger to simmering resentment but the feeling has not passed nor do I wish it to. Even as I write, my words are powered by a coursing fury. My hands hover above the keyboard in a clenched fist.

This is an anger that comes from the certainty of being. This is an anger that speaks to my soul. This anger I know to be just.

This speech tonight does not look to Lincoln's first inaugural – when the great American president spoke words of brotherhood to a fractured nation on the eve of war.

'We are not enemies but friends', he said. 'We must not be enemies. Though passion may have strained it must not break our bonds of affection.'

How I wish I could say that tonight. Another time – yes – but not tonight.

For this speech I look to Lincoln's second inaugural. Here he stood before a country bloodied and worn. Victory was at hand and slavery at an end. But this president was tired. His country lay in ruin. His assassin lurked in the audience.

Lincoln leaned on the gospels to lay at the feet of the nation the sin of slavery: 'Woe unto the world because of offences – for it must needs be that offences come, but woe to the man by whom those offences cometh.'

Woe to the man by whom those offences cometh.

What offences we have seen this past week.

How can I stand here and speak to the idea of our place in an indissoluble Commonwealth when this week my people have been reminded that our place is so often behind this nation's bars?

This week we know what Australia looks like. This week Australia is a boy in a hood strapped to a chair. This week Australia is Aboriginal boys tear-gassed, locked down and beaten. These are the images on our television screens. These boys who look like my boys.

I watched my teenage son as he saw this unfold before him. I saw him lose his place in the world, with each scene of horror he became less sure of his country. For he has been raised not to believe in our worst. He has been spared the fate of so many of his people. But on that night he wondered at the difference between himself and the boys on the screen. For in these boys he sees something of himself and he asks how his country can allow this.

When I saw the boys I saw a tragedy my son had escaped but I saw a reminder of a brutality his grandfather and my grandfather had endured. I saw in those boys the broken bones and stab wounds and dark ink jail tattoos of my father. I recalled the story of my mother's father dragged from his bed by police accused of drinking. The same man arrested and tied to a tree like a dog.

There are those who would rather I not speak of these things. There are those who accuse me of having a nostalgia for injustice. A nostalgia for injustice? As if these wounds on the body and soul of my mother and father are things of memory. As if we choose to cling to suffering, as if this injustice is a thing recalled and not a thing lived.

A nostalgia for injustice? Such a charge could be levelled only by someone certain of his place in this country. A certainty denied to a people – the First People – still searching for ours. Estranged in the land of our ancestors. It could be levelled only by someone who sees injustice and brutality as something to be pondered and not endured. It is a charge brought by people comfortable in their own history while they tell us to forget ours, to get over it.

These are people who value their traditions, exalt their heroes and deny ours. I wonder: would they dismiss the memories of the Jewish people so lightly? Are the Jewish memories of suffering too, merely a nostalgia for injustice?

These are people who proclaim themselves conservatives but with their meanness debase the very traditions they claim to uphold. These people who seize on difference – gay, Muslim, Asian, black – to vilify, divide and demonise, all the while reserving for themselves the right to define our country and set the price of inclusion. They are the people who wrap their words in civility to mask the beating heart of their bigotry.

How do these people square their supposed conservatism and professed love of country with the words of British conservative writer Roger Scruton when he says: '… individuals must be free, which means being free from the insolent claims of those who wish to redesign them'.

Yet these people seek to redesign us, to tell us who we should be and how we should think. These people would tell those boys on our television screens this week – the boys crying in agony – that they live in an imagined world of pain. They would tell them that they are to blame for their treatment.

They would tell the family of a ten-year-old Indigenous girl who takes her own life that they live in an imagined world of sadness. They would tell our people in overcrowded housing in communities ravaged by violence and drug and alcohol abuse that they revel in their misery.

They tell me I have a nostalgia for injustice.

No, we have no nostalgia for injustice because we have not first had the chance to forget.

Polish Nobel Prize-winning poet Czeslaw Milosz spoke of his people carrying the 'memory of wounds'.

… the memory of wounds – as Milosz wrote – perhaps all memory is the memory of wounds.

Certainly, for us, these memories sit deep within our soul.

Rather than long for these memories – rather than seek them out to give meaning to my identity in a perfect world – I would wish them away.

But what has been done cannot be undone. What has been seen cannot be unseen. The scars of my father and the memory of my grandfather – these stories and images – the graveyard crosses of people gone too young are seared into my mind's eyes as surely as the charred flesh and the stench of blood from a lifetime of reporting haunts my night's sleep. The memory of a hooded, bound boy in a cell is now similarly burned in my consciousness.

Australia was redeemed in part from complicity in this disgrace only by the national outrage. The prime minister responded by calling immediately for a royal commission. It may meet a minimum requirement for action but forgive us if we lack faith.

We have been poked and prodded for two centuries. We have been the subject of endless inquiry. The heads of our people rest still in glass jars in foreign museums and our skeletons contained in cardboard boxes – the artefacts of inquiry.

Two decades ago we held a royal commission into black deaths in custody; it was supposed to end the culture of incarceration. Today almost every face – man, woman and child – behind bars in the Northern Territory is black. Nationally, barely three per cent of the population comprise a quarter of those in jails.

It is not to excuse their individual crimes to make plain the fact that every one of those people – Indigenous people – are a product of this country's history. It is a history still yet to be given its full account. It is a history still yet to puncture the public consciousness. It is a history born of terra nullius – the founding of a nation on the lie of the empty land.

It is a history lamented in the 1960s by anthropologist W.E.H. Stanner as the 'Great Australian Silence'. It was, he said, 'A cult of forgetting practised on a national scale.' Half a century later his words ring just as true.

Rather than this royal commission, how more necessary is a truth and reconciliation commission. A full reckoning of our nation's past, that may set loose the chains of history that bind this country's first and today most miserably impoverished people.

In my caution I have argued against such things, fearing it would harden division. Now I accept that we need this mirror into our soul.

How can we continue to look at endemic child suicide, intractable disadvantage and our choking jail cells as mere pieces of a policy puzzle scattered on a board devoid of the outline of our troubled past?

If we are to remember the fallen of Pozieres and Fromelles, then surely we can remember the fallen warriors who resisted the invasion of their lands on this soil two hundred plus years ago.

We can remember my people the Wiradjuri and the martial law of Bathurst.

We can recall the words of one of the early settlers on the plains west of the Blue Mountains: 'It is better that all the blacks be shot and their carcasses used to manure the ground which is all the good they are fit for.'

And shot they were – and poisoned and herded over cliffs – others ravaged by disease. Half the population wiped out in a matter of years in what the *Sydney Gazette* reported as an 'exterminating war'. And this is just the story of my own blood – each of our hundreds of nations has its own similar history.

This truth telling would make good on the demand of French philosopher Paul Ricoeur: 'We must remember because remembering is a moral duty, we owe a debt to the victims.' By remembering and telling we stop them from being buried twice.

Australia's war dead are etched on walls of remembrance: 'Lest we forget'. Our dead lie in fields forgotten – histories still untold.

Without such truth where is our reconciliation? Is it just to be measured in economic statistics? Must closing the gap be the only measure of our justice? Without such truth what is this thing we are calling recognition?

I sit on the Referendum Council and this week the word itself, 'recognition', has felt small. In this week it reeks of incremental shift when we cry out for fundamental change. What is this perversity – that we should ask Australia to finally recognise us? That we should ask for others to decide whether we have a place in a constitution that was designed with our exclusion?

This recognition lives in the netherworld of symbolism when so many of the lives of our people are crushed by a real world that has never truly recognised them – that has rendered them invisible: out of sight and out of mind. We are asking Australia to recognise us when most Australians still admit to having never met an Indigenous person. They may likely hang a dot painting on their wall having never touched the hand of the painter.

This recognition doesn't speak to my father – he recognises himself when he speaks with the power of his language: still alive when Australia would have seen it silenced. Balladhu Wiradjuri Gibir – dyirramadilinya badhu Wiradjuri! I am a Wiradjuri man – proudly Wiradjuri.

In this week: how can this recognition excite our people, weary of a struggle for rights so long denied? Support for this recognition feels insipid and its supporters can speak only an air of resignation that the best we can get is less than we deserve.

I had thought that recognition may complete our nation – that it may fill the unfilled void. I saw it as a chance for Australians to recognise ourselves. I am prepared to say that I put too much store in the power of this symbolism.

Now my arguments feel timid. Recognition on these terms feels like betrayal of those who have fought for a justice more deserving, more dignified. Recognition risks shrinking our ambitions to fit a miserable national mood where the polity has lost faith in its politicians.

This recognition is hostage to politics and politics is often the enemy of the truth. This recognition demands finding common cause with those who have no interest in enlarging our nation, but containing it. This recognition demands a dispiriting compromise with those who seek to do nothing more than the least they can do.

To give full flight to our aspirations would be to court failure. What a damning state of affairs in a country that remains the only Commonwealth nation not to enshrine the sovereign rights of its First Peoples. Are we really so stricken with lethargy on this subject? Must we be comfortable with our laggard status? Do we not look to New Zealand or the United States or Canada and ask why we too cannot negotiate treaties? Treaty, even unattainable, sings to the heart of Indigenous people here in a way that recognition cannot.

If recognition is then to mean anything then we need to infuse it with the urgency of now. It needs to speak with hope to the hooded beaten boys in dark prison cells. It needs to rise above the transactions of our daily lives to sing in our hearts. It needs to whisper to the conscience of our political leaders.

If it is to mean anything it needs to be imbued with the power to reorder our lives, to give real voice to the First Peoples. If the constitution is our rulebook then we need to rewrite those rules. Anything less will speak to the poverty of our spirit not the breadth of our vision.

Can we do this? That part of me that wants to believe struggles with what my eyes this week have seen. Those boys: links in a chain that has bound us for 200 years.

This recognition: what is it without truth? To quote the poet Milosz: 'Crimes against human rights never confessed and never publicly denounced are a poison which destroys the possibility of friendship between nations.'

Can we confess these truths? My people have spoken this country's confession even when no one would listen.

Our heroes have sought to fill out this country. They have held its greatness to great account.

Our warriors of the frontier: Pemulwuy, Windradyne, Yagun, Jandamarra, Tunnerminnerwait and so many others who resisted invasion and whose names should fall from the lips of schoolchildren as easily as Captain Cook, Arthur Phillip or Ned Kelly.

Their spirit has lived in those who have followed:

Joe Anderson – otherwise known as King Burraga of the Tharawal people – who said in 1933: 'All the black man wants is representation in federal parliament. There is plenty of fish in the river for us all and land to grow all we want.'

Victorian Aboriginal leader William Cooper who in 1937 petitioned King George VI for representation in parliament.

The years have not diminished our struggle. We have fought on many fronts.

In 1963 the Yirrkala bark petitions were recognised by the Australian parliament. The Yolngu people asserted the ownership of their lands and the right to be heard.

In 1966 Vincent Lingiari walked off Wave Hill station to demand equal pay and won his land when Gough Whitlam poured the sand through Vincent's fingers.

Charles Perkins led a busload of students to smash segregation in outback New South Wales.

In 1972 a group of activists pitched a tent on the lawns of Parliament House.

In 1988 Yolngu leader Galarrwuy Yunupingu presented the Barunga statement to Prime Minister Bob Hawke demanding what the Yirrkala people had demanded in their petition to the Queen: a treaty.

Eddie Mabo, a man from Murray Island, took his battle to the highest court in the land and did not live to see his claim vindicated: this was indeed his land.

After the apology to the Stolen Generations, Galarrwuy Yunupingu gave a speech talking about what he called 'serious business': a final settlement.

Still we wait.

This week we ask again: how long do we wait?

I don't put myself in this pantheon. I live in the enormous shadow they cast. Compared to their sacrifice and leadership I feel wholly inadequate. Mine has been an individual life. I have tried to make my place in Australia.

I have tried to negotiate that compact: that you can succeed but you must not complain. This is the bargain of the successful Indigenous person: you must be an example held up as proof of Australia's racial blindness;

that anyone can make it and we must be forever grateful.

I have sought a life outside of Australia; while others battled here, I found liberation in a world where I did not have to bear the weight of our history.

This is my right. I will make those choices again. But I want to say tonight that I am indeed grateful: grateful to belong to a people who have survived. I am grateful for my parents. I am grateful to belong to a country with people who have stood with us, loved us, shared our families and fought our fight.

I will not complain. Complaining is weak. I will shout out the injustice that we have been reminded of this week.

I take no pride in the words I have spoken tonight. I don't revel in their construction. I don't wish to bask in any personal glory. I would rather I lived quietly. I would rather I didn't have to speak of what I have spoken of tonight. But these words are all I have and I am fully aware they may not be enough. They may pass into the night barely remarked.

I don't for a moment pretend that what I have said here will make a difference: many thousands of words have been spoken by people far more able and still we fail.

So I turn to words; the words of a man I turned to as I began this speech. I turn to the speech I had hoped to give. I recalled the words of Lincoln's first inaugural, his appeal to his nation's better angels. I return to the words of the weary Lincoln. The Lincoln at the start of his second term, a man whose death stalked him as he spoke:

'Let us strive on to finish the work we are in, to bind up the nation's wounds.'

Mandang Guwu – Thank you.

*

There, in that speech, were the two sides of me, my *double consciousness*. Part of me seeks to put aside rancour, to rise above resentment, the other is quick to anger, carrying the scars of Australia's history. I came to that speech consumed by rage, but by the end I could not help but appeal to hope. Irish poet William Butler Yeats wrote 'maybe a breath of politic words has withered our rose tree'. To Yeats, the time of talking is past, now 'nothing but our own red blood, can make a right rose tree'. I wonder, how do we tend the gardens of our nation? One thing I know for sure, we cannot soak our ground with the toxic water of the past.

On that night I was tethered to a history of pain; like the man of *ressentiment*, a prisoner of my past. The 'politic words' need to be spoken but they must also bring release and renewal not blame and bondage. Since that night I have asked myself if as an Aboriginal person is history all I have? Without it do I lose my identity? I have come to question the idea of 'collective memory'; memory is personal and selective. We all experience our past differently; it shapes us independently. We do *share* our pain, but it need not *define* us.

For the man of *ressentiment*, no apology, no monument, no reconciliation will ever be enough. To quote Yeats, 'he is the man whom sorrow named his friend'; ultimately all he sang was changed to an 'inarticulate moan'. He cannot fathom the difference between remembering and resentment; for him, one is impossible without the other. It is understandable: releasing the past, for him, would be a betrayal, it would be like burying his wronged ancestors twice, first their bodies and then their memories. He is caught between Homer's mythical monsters

Scylla and Charybdis, one representing remembering, the other forgetting; one is the path to anger, the other to forgiveness, and both exact a price. Forgiveness means forsaking retribution but it offers the possibility of a greater justice, peace. Philosopher Paul Ricoeur says forgiveness has a 'poetic power', it shatters 'the law of the irreversibility of time by changing the past, not as a record of all that has happened but in terms of its meaning for us today'.

Nelson Mandela and Desmond Tutu knew that forgiveness was the price they must pay to build a new nation in South Africa, free of the hatred of race. Tutu called it a 'costly business', but one lightened by a 'remarkable generosity of spirit'. Are nations only possible with forgiveness and forgetting? The nineteenth-century French philosopher and historian Ernest Renan thought so. In 1882, when in Australia it was widely presumed that Aboriginal people were a dying race, Renan penned an essay, 'What is a nation?' It remains one of the most profound and powerful statements on national identity. Renan looked beyond what he called 'the grave errors' of race, language or religion; a nation, he wrote, was defined not by any one thing but the sum of its many parts, 'the fusion of the populations that comprise them'.

Race could be no foundation for nationhood, simply because there were 'no pure races'. A nation, he wrote, was a 'soul, a spiritual principle', a marriage of the past and the present, one a 'rich trove of memories', the other 'current consent, the desire to live together, the will to value the undivided shared heritage'.

A collective identity, one free of race, language or religion; how do we find ourselves in each other when we are so tempted to look to the past and see a permanent enemy? History is the *past*, we cannot change it, but we twist it and manipulate it, we use it against each other. We turn history into a contest of triumph or suffering, history becomes a guiding star by which we sail our ships into new battles. Little wonder Ernest Renan thought the question of history was a 'threat to nationality'.

Lest we forget: each Anzac Day Australians take the solemn pledge to always remember. There is something sacred about that oath; it has become a secular liturgy. Yet the irony is not lost on Indigenous Australians, that as a nation we still find it so easy to forget the worst of our history – the massacres, the disease, segregation and discrimination. To form a nation we must choose what matters and what determines who belongs. The myth of *discovery*, the lie of terra nullius, Captain Cook, the First Fleet, Arthur Phillip, our foundation story is incomplete without also Bennelong, Pemulwuy, the Appin Massacre, the Wiradjuri wars. Australia Day lays bare the fault lines of our history and how we still face each other across the chasm of our past. History is important. It tells us who we have been. But Ernest Renan, more than a century ago, asked us something we still can't answer: why should history determine who we are?

WODORA
UDARIMJIN
GUDJI
WOLJAMDI
MINJURA
NGARINMAN
KWAI

NORTHERN

WALMANJAPARI
DJERAGI
GIGIA

MANAI

BIOOONGENA

TJI

JIKENA

NONTJANDI

LUTJA

DJARU

WA

MADALA

WULUMARI

JULBRE BUNARA

WAIADARA

WALMALA

WALPARI

BEDEDO

TEDALIA

CENTRAL

NMATJ

PINTUBI

JU MU ARA

KUKATJA

DA DADJARA

PIT JANDJARA

NANKA

ANTAK

STRALIA

MANDJINDJA

KADJARA

NADATADJARA

DIALEA

S O

LJEN

WONGAI

AUST

DGA

TJERARIDJA L

MURUNITJA

KO

MIRNID

WIR

DADJUNMA

AUSTRALIAN

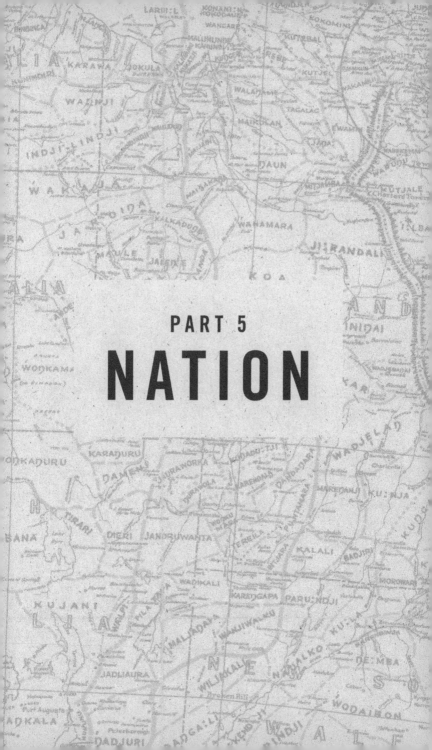

PART 5

NATION

THIRTY STEPS BETWEEN US

In 2017 I held our constitution and I felt its pull. In my hands was my country: imperfect, incomplete, indissoluble. Queen Victoria's signature of royal assent is fading: a faint reminder of how it required an Act of British Parliament to make Australia a nation. The constitution sits now protected under glass and dim light, lest the ravages of air and time erase it. Rarely is it removed. I held it aware of the privilege. I have a romantic disposition, an affection for tradition and reverence for antiquity, and with that yellowed and weathered document removed from its protective glass casing and resting in my hand, it held a powerful resonance.

Our constitution speaks to our resolve, our endurance, the strength of our democracy. The words of our founding document carry a heavy load. These words come from a time of great debate when a people sought to lift their gaze from parochialism to find amity; out of difference to find union.

These words speak from our past, define our present and underwrite our future. As these words gave shape to a new Commonwealth so they allowed for a Commonwealth still to come: a dynamic nation, a reforming nation. In its final section, section 128, the constitution enshrines the capacity for its own alteration. Change can come only from the people in a referendum carried by a majority of voters in a majority of states.

It is a formidable requirement. In forty-four referenda put before the people, on only eight occasions has there been successful carriage. On the day I held our constitution I held, too, the most resoundingly approved amendment. In my hand was the Constitution Alteration (Aboriginals) 1967. It won 90.77 per cent of votes cast and carried in all six states. It is a phenomenal achievement, that a handful of Aboriginal people could form a movement, win others to their side and change forever this nation. There is much talk about the racism of our country, and it is true it is a stain on our soul, but when tested, Australians have raised their sights. The referendum altered both provisions in which Aboriginal people were mentioned. Section 51 (xxvi) was amended to give power to the federal government to make laws for Aboriginal people, and it struck out section 127 which had had excluded Aboriginal people from being counted in the census.

In my right hand was the Australian Constitution, in my left the most potent example of the power to change it. In my left hand was a milestone in the journey of my people. Here was the struggle to be heard; the struggle to be counted. As the constitution spoke to me of the enduring strength of Australia's foundation, so it spoke to me too of the subjugation of my people. As part of me could feel a pride in the creation of Australia, another part of me felt a deep conflict. Let us not forget that at the birth of our modern nation, the First Peoples of this land were deemed unfit to be counted. There was no voice of the First Peoples in our constitution's draft.

The 1967 referendum was a watershed moment for Australia; it is a high point in the relationship between black and white; one of those rare moments when as nation we spoke almost as one. Yet it remains a victory half won. If anything it ushered in a new era of struggle, as Aboriginal people stepped up the struggle to be recognised in their own country.

I crossed the hallway from the room in which the constitution is preserved to another room which holds the inalienable aspirations of Indigenous people. I counted the steps; just 30. Thirty steps from the constitution to the Larrakia Petition. It reads: 'Gwalwa Daraniki – This is our land.' This petition by the Larrakia people of the Northern Territory gathered more than a thousand signatures from Aboriginal people across Australia and was delivered to the Queen in 1972. It is torn and frayed but it speaks to me with a power still undiminished; a demand so just, so clear and still so denied.

> The British settlers took our land. No treaties were signed
> with the tribes. Today we are REFUGEES. Refugees in the
> country of our ancestors. We live in REFUGEE CAMPS
> without land, without employment, without justice.

The petition called for treaties like those of the Maoris of New Zealand and the Native Americans. The names of the signatories are scratched on the document, some marked it with their thumb prints. Whole communities signed with the names of their towns. I looked closely and found mine: Griffith, New South Wales. From the constitution to the Larrakia Petition: thirty steps that count the distance between me and my nation, Australia.

Where is the road map for that journey? Professors Megan Davis and Marcia Langton in their introduction to a collection of essays from Indigenous leaders, *It's Our Country*, write:

> There are two paths from here. One is the path of listening
> and not hearing. And the other is the path of listening and
> hearing.

But what are Indigenous people saying? Marcia Langton looks to the continuing reference to race in our constitution and sees self-loathing, dehumanisation, and complicity in racism. Barrister Tony McAvoy sees the belief that Australia was legitimately settled as an immovable rock from which governments and the people cannot move. To go forward, he writes, Indigenous people are crucial to the process. He advocates an assembly of first nations to negotiate eventual treaties.

Geoff Scott – a long-time senior bureaucrat and advocate – calls for substantive reform that acknowledges our uniqueness and difference and moves beyond just a call for equality for all. To lawyer Michael Mansell, 'recognise' is a strange word; it acknowledges the obvious, Aboriginal people were always here. He favours legislation enshrining the distinct rights of Indigenous people. Megan Davis argues that how the British asserted sovereignty over the land – extinguishing Indigenous rights, rendering them British subjects – means this is unfinished business. But she also concedes Indigenous people are divided over how to finish that business: 'a principled resistance camp, a resistance-to-anything camp, wait-and-see camp and a not yet camp'.

Differences aside, all wrestle with the same question: how to live as people with rights and dignity in a country that has historically denied – or not even recognised – those rights. Contrast the range of Indigenous positions with those of interested, engaged non-Indigenous thinkers. In a companion publication, *The Forgotten People*, a range of conservative writers, jurists, academics and religious figures offer their ideas for recognition. They are uniformly of generous spirit and compassion. There is a deep sense of the need to redress how our nation has failed its first peoples.

Lawyer and philosopher Damien Freeman says the time has come to recognise that successive generations of the Crown's representatives have failed to treat Indigenous people fairly. He believes Australians have come to understand and share the deep attachment of the first nations to this continent and that this could underpin a settlement. Columnist Chris Kenny too speaks of a spiritual attachment to this home – Australia – that allows him to imagine an Indigenous sense of estrangement in the land of our ancestors. He looks for a resolution that is conservative, practical and an end point to historical grievance. Law professor Greg Craven is supportive too but counsels the political realities: 'practicality is the kissing cousin to substance'. Ambition is fine, but the perfect can be the enemy of the good. Indigenous politics, like all politics, is the art of the possible.

There are arguments of morality and fairness and justice. The more creative support models such as that proposed by Indigenous advocate Noel Pearson for a representative advisory body to help shape Indigenous policy. Pearson argues that Indigenous people need to find a 'hook' in the constitution on which to hang their aspirations and demands.

Generally though, the non-Indigenous thinkers are cautious. Their support is framed around unity and reconciliation. As Damien Freeman writes, recognition may present an opportunity but reform of the constitution also risks

threatening its backbone. Former Human Rights Commissioner
now Federal Liberal MP, Tim Wilson, argues it can help shape
Australians' aspirations for our shared vision of our nation. But
he warns of disconnect between the aspirations of Indigenous
people and the rest of Australia. Misgivings notwithstanding,
conservative support is essential to any political outcome. To
Noel Pearson a successful recognition referendum hinges on
this backing. The political realities of passing any such national
poll suggest he is right.

But the measured tone of the conservatives speaks to their
comfort in an Australia that has never excluded them. The
urgency and passion and dignity and righteousness of the
Indigenous advocates comes from those who know the sting of
dispossession and injustice. The first peoples draw from a great
well of sadness. It is a history of loss: lives singed by the fires of
poverty and bigotry.

At times of great national occasion I confess to often feeling
hollow. There is a hole where my country should be. When I held
the Australian Constitution I felt a great reverence. When I
looked upon the Larrakia Petition I felt belonging. The measure
of our country is when these great documents speak equally to us
all. But how do we close those thirty steps? Individuals have
reached across that divide and have found a sense of shared
belonging. Families have been born out of that love between us
that defies a history of segregation. Aboriginal people have
looked for a place in a country – their country – even as it was
denied them.

Treaty, recognition: these are the things that can help
complete a nation. Beyond the legalese and the politics, they
could form the lyrics of a song of our country. They should speak

not to separatism and unending grievance but to the 'serious business' of healing the 'memory of wounds', resolving the Australian settlement and connecting us all – descendants of the First Peoples or the most recent refugee – to what it is to be an Australian; to fill those thirty steps between us.

THE CUNNING OF
RECOGNITION

A nation is a grand lie, a thing of fiction; you could say it is entirely a mirage, something we imagine into being. There is nothing natural about nations, they are not ordained by God or handed down from our ancestors. Secular nations are a modern invention, they were born in blood, emerging from rebellion against a time when we were ruled by monarchies or religious leaders. The world as we know it took root in the seventeenth-century treaty of Westphalia (1648), marking the end of the Thirty Years War – that left at least eight million people dead. A new political order was created, one of sovereignty and independence. States pledged to stay out of each other's affairs.

Aboriginal people would have had no way of knowing what was happening in Europe, how the people of an entire continent had torn themselves apart to put themselves together again. It is impossible to be sure today, but before the British claimed this land there were thought to be anywhere from 250 to 700 distinct groups here. Today, we call them nations, adopting that European term to describe the tribes and clan groups that lived here bounded by their own borders and linked by trade and ceremony. More than a century after the warring tribes of Europe came together, Captain Cook planted a flag that sowed the seeds for a new nation that would become Australia.

Flags don't make a nation. Guns and ships don't make a nation. Politicians can write constitutions but a nation is more than a set of laws. What is it that binds people together, that is stronger than our instinct to turn on each other? In 1983 sociologist Benedict Anderson unlocked this secret. The most powerful unifying force among us was speech, language; our words gave meaning to nation. He called it a 'consciousness of connectedness'. Before the treaty of Westphalia, a revolution was already underway; a revolution of language that unleashed a fire in the mind. The printing press had already put information into the hands of ordinary people; literacy improved; stories could be shared quickly and widely. This created a potent sense of shared destiny that trumped other affiliations – race, culture, religion – that may have otherwise divided people. As Anderson wrote, '… one can sleep with anyone, but one can only read some people's words'.

That's what a nation is: a story. Stories are how we explain ourselves to each other. It is a story that we imbibe, and a story we so rarely question. What is our story? It is terra nullius. Historian Stuart Macintyre calls it a story of 'a sleeping land finally brought to life'. It is a British story – a white story. Look at the names we gave our cities: Sydney, Melbourne, Perth, Hobart, all named after British politicians; Adelaide is named after a queen and Brisbane, a governor. But I've long thought there is something else lurking in Australia, a trace of a story much older that holds us in its grip even as we have sought to deny it. Look at the names of farms and properties in Australia, think again about our rural towns; so many of them have Aboriginal names.

Where I grew up there was Narrandera, Wagga Wagga, Cootamundra, Gundagai; it was as if the settlers were reminding themselves whose land this was even as the local people were being forced off.

A sleeping land, brought to life – empty land – the legal fiction struck down by the High Court in the *Mabo* decision, but so deeply lodged in the Australian consciousness that for much of this nation's history it rendered Indigenous people invisible. Terra nullius gave the British licence to write their own story here. In her book *Being Australian*, sociologist Catriona Elder speaks of the 'terra nullius narrative' – a white story written in an empty space. Elder says the 'terra nullius story meant non-Indigenous peoples could imagine they were telling a story where no other story existed'. It is a story that did not include my black ancestors. Their presence countered the European claim on this land, a reminder of a deeper sense of belonging here. They were depicted as the 'noble savage' or the 'doomed race' bound for extinction. As Elder says, a people who 'could not survive the inevitable onslaught of a modern world'.

Australia in many ways has been perplexed by Aboriginal survival. Extinction, segregation and assimilation have all been predicated on disappearance – a people fading away on the margins or 'absorbed' into the Commonwealth. Elder says, 'Indigeneity or blackness is excluded from the nation by Indigenous peoples being made white.' What remains is an enduring and frustrating question of authenticity. Who are the 'real Aborigines'?

Anthropologist Elizabeth Povinelli says Indigenous Australians are forced 'to identify with the impossible object of an authentic identity'. It is still true that most Australians have never met an Indigenous person and may be utterly unaware if they had. People like me – urban, mixed race, middle class – appear like any other Australian; another face on our multi-ethnic streets. Povinelli says Australia is unnerved by the claims of people who are so familiar, yet so strange; people 'hauntingly similar to themselves', who 'dress, act and sound like the suburban neighbours they are'.

In her book *The Cunning of Recognition,* Povinelli explores that space where race and Indigenous rights meets political liberalism. When it comes to recognition, she asks just what or who is the nation in fact *recognising*? She questions if Australia is serious about the *rights* and *place* of Aboriginal people in our nation, or if recognition is a shortcut to *whitewashing* our history? Is it in truth less about justice than easing Australia's national conscience? Povinelli takes aim at the holy grail of Australian legal history, the *Mabo* High Court judgment overturning terra nullius and ushering in native title. This is rightly regarded as a high point of Australian liberalism, a milestone of reconciliation. The judges themselves made it clear that the case was an opportunity to cleanse the nation's collective sin. But Povinelli, who worked among Indigenous communities for almost two decades, wonders exactly where Aboriginal people fit into this new story 'of national identity, of history, and consciousness'.

Amid the celebrations of the *Mabo* decision, Povinelli says we missed what was really happening; this was always more about rehabilitating the Australian nation than recognising the rights of the First Peoples. What was at stake, she said, 'was not simply a nation's shame at its past as a coloniser. At stake was its future.' There was a trade-off, Australian law would recognise the *limited* rights of Aboriginal people and in return those same Aboriginal people would release Australia from its guilt. Povinelli calls it a 'liberal imaginary' where Indigenous Australians would 'slough off their traumatic histories, ambivalences, incoherencies, and angst like so much outgrown skin'.

Recognition has always appeared to me to ask more of black people than white, Aboriginal people feel strongly the expectations that they will forgive their fellow Australians. Recognition is linked to the desire for reconciliation – one can't exist without the other. Yet reconciliation has always been a flawed project, it emerged in the 1990s out of political failure, the decision by the Hawke Labor government to backtrack on a promised treaty. Questions of sovereignty and legal and political rights for First Peoples would instead be replaced by gestures of national *healing*, and closing the socioeconomic gap.

Fast forward two decades and Indigenous people have grown impatient with progress, it is what fuels the anger we see on our streets each Australia Day. Reconciliation and recognition have become bywords for assimilation, the political equivalent of beads and trinkets. In a public lecture in 2018, Yawuru leader, Peter Yu – a long-time champion of Aboriginal rights and a pragmatic and thoughtful man – was reduced to despair. Reconciliation, he said, with a commitment to a full political settlement 'no longer exists', it has 'lost its moral and political gravitas'. As a nation, we have traded substance for symbolism. This was a devastating appraisal of the abject failure of Australia to heal its deepest wound, while Indigenous people continued to fill our prisons and cemeteries. In spite of it all, like me, Peter Yu maintains a faith in the goodness of Australian people 'far better than the political system which represents us'. What is at stake is Australia's 'moral and ethical national character'.

Our national story: a sleeping land brought to life; a restless land; a nation unfinished. There is a deep unease here: *uncanny* – a place familiar but strange. As I have written in this book, our art and literature and film probe that question of *being at home*. All that we have built; all of our laws; 200 years and we can't quite shake it – that thing that dwells in us: we don't really belong. It's there in the surge in popularity of outback crime novels; Chris Hammer's *Scrublands* and Jane Harper's *The Dry* take us again to that *vanishing place*; the dark foreboding bush that swallows us up. We cannot separate the land from murder. But when we put down our books we return to our daily lives of family, work, school and sport, and push aside those dark thoughts. It is a privilege that other Australians enjoy. I wonder what it must be like to know contentment. It eludes me. Modern Australia was not built for Aboriginal people, my black ancestors were expected not even to survive. Australia is a British invention, conceived by Britain initially for British – *white* – people: a far-flung outpost of empire. I was talking to a prominent Aboriginal leader once and he turned to me with a look of loss; a moment of feeling defeated and deflated. 'It is their country now,' he said.

I am caught in the crosshairs of Australian freedom; as an individual I have been able to pursue my dreams yet there are those in my family for whom freedom itself remains a dream.

In a multicultural society Indigenous people feel the strains of belonging on the one hand, and on the other clinging to culture and identity; not a blended part of Australia but a people distinct and unique. The state has historically determined who is or is not Aboriginal, and now, to prove native title, they must prove who they are all over again. It is the state that decides which customs and laws of Indigenous society it finds worthy or acceptable, and Indigenous people must conform, as Povinelli says, to 'gain access to public sympathy and state resources'. This is what she calls the 'cunning of recognition', an act of acknowledgment that may be more about protecting and enhancing the honour of the wider society – Australia – than in truly seeing the very people it is meant to be recognising – Indigenous people.

So, where are we? Australia has been framed by terra nullius, and Indigenous people locked in the imagination of a nation that has throughout its history, too often found the black presence uncomfortable or offensive. Now those same Indigenous people must prove their authenticity. Australian society sets the boundaries. I often feel torn between belonging to Australia and being an Indigenous person. I live with that tension. It is the curse of the outsider.

What remains, for me, is the hope of liberalism. Scholars like Elizabeth Povinelli are right to wonder if Australian liberal democracy, its rule of law, can ever truly speak equally to Indigenous people, but it is not something I am ready to give up on. Liberalism is a fighting faith and right now it needs its defenders. Around our world the liberal order is being challenged in new ways by rising authoritarianism, poor leadership and a loss of trust in the institutions of democracy. In Australia we face our own battles: our own reckoning with the 'End of History'.

WE ARE NOW ONE PEOPLE

The words we use to hide our shame, think about them: *dispossessed* instead of *stolen*; *settled* not *invaded*; *explorers* who were really *intruders*. We have crafted a new language to tell the story of Australia because we are damned by the truth. We can't yet bring ourselves to say *massacre* or *war* let alone *genocide*. Why do we refer to a people who had lived here longer than human memory as *custodians* of the land? Because *owners* have rights.

Here is the question that for two centuries has haunted Australia: whose country is this? Sixty-five thousand years cannot be so easily erased. There was no treaty, no deed of title, no conveyancing; there was just a flag claiming for Britain ownership of an *empty land*. Surely this is done; this is settled; but not for Indigenous people. This is Australia's unfinished business.

Australia exists on a skeleton of law, the bare bones of legal judgments that refuse to accept the First Peoples of this continent as *sovereign* people. Terra nullius has been struck down, the High Court accepts the obvious that when Captain Cook arrived there were people here. But the judges in the historic *Mabo* case would not disturb the grounds of Australian *settlement*. They would not entertain the idea that the Crown's possession of this land is illegal. But *Mabo* was just the latest in a string of legal challenges to British sovereignty stretching back two centuries. Most Australians would be utterly unaware of this history, and we are poorer because of it. I came to this thinking I would be buried in opaque legalese, bogged down in mind numbing technical points of law. How wrong I was. Here are cases of murder, political power struggles and rebel judges prepared to speak against the law of their own land. What is revealed is another Australia entirely, a shadowland where all the things we believe to be true, shatter.

We have to go back to 1836, when Aboriginal man Jack Murrell was charged with murder. His lawyers decided to turn it into a test case: here was an opening to overturn the very foundation of the colony. They argued that Murrell was not a British subject, and British law did not apply to him. They said he could be judged only under his customary tribal law. The Chief Justice of the New South Wales Supreme Court was interested enough to describe the argument as an 'ingenious defence', but he rejected it. As far as he was concerned everyone – Aborigines included – was subject to the Crown. This ruling set a precedent that continues today; in Australian law, Aboriginal sovereignty was extinguished.

Yet back in Britain, the matter was far from finished. Politicians of the day debated just what right the Crown had to take the land of Indigenous people. In 1837, the Select Committee of the House of Commons on Aborigines produced a remarkable statement that held: 'The land has been taken from them without the assertion of any title than that of a superior force ...'

By 1841, the issue was back in the Supreme Court of New South Wales. Justice John Walpole Willis said 'in Australia it is the colonists not the Aborigines who are the foreigners'. Justice

Willis was presiding on a case that threatened to upend all the assumptions of British ownership of this land. The case, still taught in law schools today, is known as *R v Bonjon* (1841), it involved a young Aboriginal man accused of murdering another Aboriginal man over a customary law tribal marriage dispute. It quickly promised to become more than a murder trial: the colony itself was in the dock.

Justice Willis's opening address ran to 8000 words and took over three hours to read out, describing the British, as 'uninvited intruders'. He said that the 'Aborigines must be considered and dealt with ... as distinct, though dependent tribes governed by themselves'. Aboriginal people, he said, should be seen 'either as the sovereigns or proprietors of the soil'. The settlers, he said, knew that 'every part of this territory was the undisputed property of the aborigines'.

Justice Willis even lamented the lack of a treaty and that there were 'no terms defined for their internal government, civilisation and protection'. The judge argued that British settlement was an unlawful act that did not extinguish Aboriginal sovereignty and that sovereignty remained intact. It was a remarkable statement from the bench, which claimed Aboriginal peoples were domestic dependent nations and that disputes among Aboriginal people should be governed by 'their own rude laws and customs'. Justice Willis questioned whether he could even exercise jurisdiction, the case was ultimately abandoned and *R v Bonjon*, has never received the attention it could have. The defendant, Bonjon, was released but within a few years was dead, killed in a tribal revenge attack. Justice Willis ultimately fell foul of the political powers that be and was dismissed as a judge. Governor Sir George Gipps cited the *Bonjon* case among others as reasons for dismissing

Willis, characterised as 'errors in law, or of what I can only designate as his attempts to produce mischief'.

The question of Aboriginal rights and sovereignty was fiercely contested in the nineteenth century. In 1841 the British Privy Council ruled that New South Wales had been regarded as 'a tract of territory, practically unoccupied, without settled inhabitants or settled land, at the time when it was peacefully annexed to the British dominions'.

The British law lords had slammed shut the book on the rights of Aboriginal people. This forms what is known today as the *skeleton of Australian law*. No court has overturned it, despite case after case disputing the legitimacy of the Crown. In 1971, the Yolngu people of Arnhem Land took on the might of the mining company Nabalco, which had secured a twelve-year bauxite mining lease. The Yolngu said it was their land; they were the sovereigns. *Milirrpum v Nabalco*, as it is known, was the first time in Australia a court would have to rule on native title.

Would this be it? This time, would an Australian judge confirm what Aboriginal people had never stopped believing: that they were no one's *subject*? If any people were a sovereign people surely it was the Yolngu. They spoke their own language; they practised ceremonies, told ancient stories; and were governed by the laws of their ancestors. Song, dance, art, politics, trade: nothing here was inherited from Britain. Wouldn't the court see this? This was indeed a landmark case, Justice Richard Blackburn went where no Australian judge had gone – further even than Justice Willis a century before. Justice Blackburn recognised that the Yolngu had a civilisation as sure as any on earth. Aboriginal people, he found, had a 'subtle and elaborate system of law … if ever a system could be called a government of law … it is shown in evidence before me'.

There was a glimmer of hope. But Justice Blackburn like others before him would not upend the foundation of this country. Ultimately he ruled that this land was a 'desert and uncultivated'. Aboriginal people had been usurped by British sovereignty, they had no claim on this land. Australia, he said, was indeed a 'settled colony'.

Paul Coe was a former footballer and a young law student in 1979, when he lodged a case in the High Court to challenge Australian sovereignty. Coe had grown up on the Erambie Aboriginal reserve in the New South Wales town of Cowra, it was a tough place and he'd seen racism and brutality first hand. Coe lodged his case on behalf of the Wiradjuri – the biggest Aboriginal group in eastern Australia, claiming that like the Yolngu, his people had their own laws and traditions and had never ceded their land to Britain. *Coe v The Commonwealth* was ultimately dismissed, the judges ruled that it was a poorly drafted statement of claim, but not before Justice Murphy rattled the bones of old Australia.

> ... the aborigines did not give up their lands peacefully; they
> were killed or removed forcibly from the lands by United
> Kingdom forces or the European colonists in what amounted
> to attempted (and in Tasmania almost complete) genocide.
> The statement by the Privy Council may be regarded either
> as having been made in ignorance or as a convenient
> falsehood to justify the taking of aborigines' land.

All roads lead eventually to the *Mabo* case. In a poetic piece of irony Torres Strait Islander man Eddie Mabo was a gardener at Townsville's James Cook University when he took on the legacy of Captain Cook himself. He was defeated at every turn but fought all the way to the High Court to overturn the doctrine of terra nullius. The Mabo decision was indeed historic, perhaps the most important legal judgment in Australian history. The judges found that a people were here when the British arrived, this was not an 'empty land'. When Captain Cook planted the British flag in this land, native title fell to the soil with the laws of the Crown.

But Aboriginal people hoping to settle the question of sovereignty were again disappointed. The justices took their lead from that old Privy Council ruling from 1841, the law would not budge from the belief that this land was 'peacefully annexed'. In the words of Justice Brennan, the court could not 'fracture the skeleton' of our law.

When Captain Cook arrived on these shores in 1770, he came with *secret instructions*. The *Endeavour* was officially on a voyage of science to observe the transit of Venus, but there was another mission. The king's orders were to 'make discovery' of the great south continent. The king was explicit, Cook was to 'cultivate a friendship and alliance' with the 'natives'. He was to take possession of this land 'with the consent of the natives'. Consent was not sought let alone given. More than two centuries later Aboriginal people are yet to consent.

By the eighteenth century the world was coming, Aboriginal people were never going to remain in isolation. Dutch navigator, Willem Janszoon, had explored the western and southern coasts more than 150 years before Cook arrived. Macassans were visiting the north and trading with local people by the early 1700s. It was inevitable that soon the boats would come to stay. We cannot turn back time, Aboriginal people cannot wish away the past 200 years. But we are a haunted nation; tormented still by that first injustice from which all other injustices flow. Our writers, our storytellers and artists, our judges know this and in our bones we – all of us who call this place home – know it too.

Settled or conquered? It is a critical question, that reveals perhaps why our history books for so long left blank the pages of the frontier wars when black and white fought hard and long over this land. If Australia was indeed conquered, international law tells us that the rights of the so-called 'conquered people' would remain. British common law is elastic. That is one of its strengths, it changes to fit the new realities on the ground. It absorbs the laws of the conquered peoples. This helps explain countries like New Zealand, a British settlement that continues to recognise the sovereignty of the Maori people.

New Zealand was never deemed empty; the Maori were recognised and the battles they fought against the British form the story of the nation. In 1840, Maori chiefs signed the Treaty of Waitangi, what New Zealand calls its founding document. At the treaty ceremony British Lieutenant Governor, William Hobson, is said to have remarked in Maori language, 'He iwi tahi tatou' – 'We are now one people'. That could have been us; we could have written such a different story for ourselves. It tears at us still, I know because I carry that conflict deep inside me. We live together and we love each other. We have fought each other and fought in wars alongside each other. Remember we – black and white danced together briefly under the stars on the beach when the First Fleet weighed anchor. But there is that space between us. It is our birth stain, our original sin, it is what stops us too finally being able to say, 'We are now one people.'

THE TORMENT OF
POWERLESSNESS

In 2007, the military rolled into an Australian town. Mutitjulu, a small Indigenous community in the shadow of our nation's spiritual heart, Uluru, was now ground zero in what would become known as 'the intervention'. A decade later, in 2017, the nation's Indigenous leadership stood on that same ground to ask for a new relationship with Australia: the Uluru Statement from the Heart.

Between those two events is what W.E.H. Stanner once dubbed the 'torment of powerlessness'. Here is the story of the First Peoples of this land living with the weight of history, the burden of colonisation, the misery of poverty.

This is the depressingly familiar narrative played out time and again in our media: communities tormented by the wailing of funeral ceremonies and the cries of children and mothers.

Those cries are lost in a political process that does not hear the ambitions and aspirations of Indigenous people. The failure to listen, the refusal to talk was a hallmark of the intervention.

This was Prime Minister John Howard's declared emergency. It was a time of fear and suspicion, of claims of 'paedophile rings', rampant abuse and communities awash in drugs and alcohol.

What started at Mutitjulu spread to scores of other communities. There were reports of Aboriginal families fleeing as the troops came in. The mayor of Mount Isa in Queensland asked for help to deal with an influx of Aboriginal people coming from the Northern Territory.

It is remembered by many Indigenous people as a dark time. Indigenous leader and health expert Pat Turner laments the intervention as a 'complete violation of the human rights of Aboriginal people'. It was officially termed the Northern Territory Emergency Response, a half-billion-dollar package to impose new controls on black communities.

More police were deployed, curfews were imposed, there were bans on alcohol and restrictions on welfare payments.

Indigenous lease arrangements were overhauled and the government suspended the permit system controlling access to communities. The soldiers were on hand to assist in logistics and implementation but their presence was a symbolic reminder of colonisation and the often-fractious relationship between Aboriginal people and the state.

When Australians voted in overwhelming numbers in 1967 to give Indigenous people a 'fair go' in this country, I doubt they had this in mind. But the intervention is the by-product of those good intentions. The 1967 referendum for the first time gave power to the federal government to make laws for Aboriginal people.

In 2007 the Howard government overrode the Northern Territory government and set aside sections of the *Racial Discrimination Act* to intervene directly into the lives of Indigenous people. This issue of control sits at the heart of the push for a new referendum to recognise Indigenous people in the constitution. It is about completing 1967.

In 2017 Indigenous leaders issued a cry from the heart. The Uluru Statement, as it has become known, spoke to powerlessness. It was a call for an 'ancient sovereignty' that would shine as a 'fuller expression of Australia's nationhood'.

The statement said, 'proportionately, we are the most incarcerated people on the planet. We are not an innately criminal people.' It spoke of children alienated from their families; children should be 'our hope for the future'.

The dimensions of the crisis, the statement said, revealed a structural problem. Only through rewriting our nation's founding document, the constitution, could we right the wrongs. Only then could Aboriginal people take a 'rightful place in our own country.'

The Indigenous leaders called for a new 'voice' – a representative body – that would speak for the powerless. In the words of Noel Pearson – one of the architects of the Uluru Statement – Indigenous Australians needed an Australian 'shield' that would defend against the sword of potentially harmful government legislation.

In his 2014 *Quarterly Essay* 'A Rightful Place', Pearson challenged Australia as to whether its 'system of democracy enables an extreme minority to participate in a fair way.' Pearson wrote:

> The scale and moral urgency of the Indigenous predicament far exceeds the power of Indigenous participation in the country's democratic process.

Pearson had belled the cat. Here was the fundamental question of Australia, it is the question that turns over and over in my mind –

it is the question that has hovered over my every thought in this book – is liberalism a big enough idea to liberate me from the chokehold of race, identity and history? If liberalism works for others, can it work for me?

The Uluru Statement is a leap of faith. It is asking Indigenous people to sign on to the idea of Australia, the *land of dreams*. Yet there is deep scepticism – even hostility – to Australian democracy; to liberalism. Indigenous people are told that we should all be *individuals*; that justice must be colour-blind, that we are *all the same*, we should all just be Australians. How much easier that is for those whose lives have been untouched by the legacy of racism and segregation. Liberalism asks easier questions of white people; it poses tougher questions of someone like me. I have to work harder to embrace it; I have to push the limits of liberalism until it bends to include me.

I'm not alone, there are black writers and thinkers from different parts of the world committed to political liberalism but fully aware that it has historically worked against them. It is a high-wire act if black people get too close to liberalism, they can become radioactive. They are accused by other blacks, as 'thinking white:' you're a sell-out or worse, an Uncle Tom. To some beyond redemption. But there are those like Caribbean scholar Charles Mills who are writing their own redemption song. He doesn't want to throw out liberalism, but prise it open, get inside it and shake it up. He doesn't hold back, liberalism has a 'race problem', it is shaped by 'white supremacy'. Liberals need to find a new way to talk to minorities in society, he says, they must accept 'black rights and white wrongs'.

Mills is staring down those old giants of philosophy – dead white men – and turning their own arguments against them. Did

Immanuel Kant, John Locke or David Hume truly believe in fairness? Did they seek justice for all people or did they mean white people? Today we would call Kant a racist: he said openly that black people are stupid. Liberals like to think they are beyond racism, but it is baked in hard. Now they tell us we should put race aside, stop playing the race card. How they love repeating Martin Luther King Jnr – that we should judge people by the content of their character not the colour of their skin. They forget that King was dreaming.

We can't just level the playing field, outlawing discrimination is not enough. We cannot all live under a veil of ignorance unaware of each other's race, gender, class, sexuality, religion. How can the rules of the game apply equally to us all when not all have been treated equally? Mills says this ideal world has never existed; no individual was enslaved, blacks were bought and sold as a group; we can't pretend to be colour-blind today. A just future means first undoing the injustice of the past.

Liberalism is a philosophy of progress, it doesn't cope well with the past. Liberal democracies are the same the world over, we are no different; they are much more comfortable with the things unsaid than the harsh truth. Liberalism is flawed, it has been complicit in racism and colonisation. Yet for all of that it is a glorious idea, a dream of freedom: *the End of History.* If history is the struggle to break free of our chains then liberalism is the final destination. Am I being too romantic; too misty-eyed? Perhaps. But I have seen the alternative. I have lived and worked in countries that crush freedom; that jail those who protest or speak out; countries where Big Brother is always watching. If I could write a love letter to liberalism, freedom is what I would cherish most.

Rather than reject liberalism we need to open up new pathways to justice for those whom liberalism has traditionally excluded or ignored. Liberalism's cherished belief in *individual rights* can be compatible with *group rights*. The towering political thinker of the twentieth century was the American John Rawls; he rewrote the book on justice and fairness. Rawls believed in a 'civic friendship' built among people with 'disparate aims' but who recognise 'a shared conception of justice'. Put simply, we may disagree with the road map but agree on the destination.

Rawls lit a fire among a new generation of philosophers black and white, who try to square the circle of liberalism and the legacy of history. African-American, Tommie Shelby, says we can pursue justice without reverting to the divisive politics of identity. He walks a delicate line between what he calls '*thick*' and '*thin*' *blackness*. As the labels imply, *thick blackness* emphasises *racial solidarity*; *thin blackness* puts the emphasis on *justice*. It is a subtle but crucial distinction, that acknowledges how blacks collectively can unite in the pursuit of their rights but not be forever bound by exclusive notions of black racial identity. He, more even than Charles Mills, has spoken most powerfully to me, particularly his belief that 'black individuals are the primary units of moral concern': when the oppressed group is liberated, the individual is set free.

Duncan Ivison, who I mentioned in my doctoral confirmation speech to the University of New South Wales, says we need a 'post-colonial liberalism'. He asks if 'liberal democracy can become genuinely intercultural?' Ivison navigates that narrow passage between Indigenous rights and the legitimacy of the colonial state. Aboriginal people have been angered by Australia's refusal – legally and politically – to acknowledge enduring

Indigenous sovereignty, which they say has never been ceded. Historically British and later Australian law claimed to extinguish Aboriginal sovereignty, but Ivison has tried to untie this Gordian knot. Other countries – Canada, America, New Zealand – have recognised *dependent sovereignty* where pre-existing nations now subsumed by modern secular states still maintain degrees of self-determination. Ivison asks, why not us? He says Australia needs to create a 'mutually acceptable coexistence'. Rather than the problem, Ivison sees liberalism as the answer; a more innovative liberalism that 'can be taken hold of, translated and renewed'.

Liberalism, for me, is the paper on which I can write my own peace with Australia. Thinkers like Tommie Shelby, Charles Mills and Duncan Ivison lift the blinkers from my eyes and allow me to imagine liberal democracy anew. I can see how those excluded – like my family – can find a way in. The Ghanaian-British philosopher Kwame Anthony Appiah says modern liberalism can not be blind to difference; identity, he says, 'is at the heart of human life'. The trick for liberalism is 'to construct a state and society that takes this account of the ethics of identity without losing sight of the values of personal autonomy'.

This is an important debate for Australia to have. Philosophy matters; ideas are the engine of progress. The clash of ideas has sparked revolution and war. Today, thirty years after post-Cold War assumptions of the *End of History*, liberalism thought to be triumphant and transcendent, is under renewed attack. The West is facing an identity crisis, no longer sure of itself. There is a loss of faith in institutions – banks, the church, political parties – exacerbated by growing inequality and rapid technological change. Far from the promised nirvana of open borders, free trade and free movement of people, we have seen borders going back up and a resistance to immigration, especially refugees. Political populists – left and right – are exploring fear and anxieties stoking a resurgent tribal warfare: identity is the buzzword of today. Democracy itself is in retreat, in Australia a survey by the influential think-tank, the Lowy Institute, found that a third of young people here no longer believe democracy is the best form of government.

The West is battered and tired. The United States is showing signs of retreat, its global leadership and prestige worn down by endless war in Afghanistan and Iraq. The shadows of the attacks of 11 September 2001 orchestrated by Osama bin Laden's al-Qaeda, loom long. It shook America's confidence and has tested its resolve. It has drained the US of blood and treasure. The Global Financial Crisis – a worldwide recession if not depression – has shattered confidence in the global economy; the rules of the game looked rigged; the entire financial system exposed as an elaborate shell game. Ordinary Americans lost their houses and livelihoods and the shock waves have been felt around the globe. And all of this is playing out at a time when China – an authoritarian still-Marxist regime – represents a viable and worrying alternative to what we call the liberal democratic order. It is little wonder some are asking, *has the West lost it?*

Don't think for a moment that this doesn't affect Indigenous issues; Indigenous people are in the crosshairs of this global crisis. The anger and protest on Australia Day is part of this growing resentment, liberal democracy has left a bitter taste in the mouths of many Aboriginal people. If liberalism is to survive it will need to meet this challenge here and abroad. Liberalism is a fighting faith, and we need to plant our flag firmly in the ground.

But this is not a discussion we are good at here. Too quickly any attempt to square the legacy of history with the future of liberalism descends into a culture war between those who want to dismantle the West and others pledged to defend it. Western triumphalists are frozen solid in an eighteenth-century vision of Enlightenment and Liberalism that is ill equipped to deal with the complexity of challenges in a diverse, interconnected world. Enlightenment was never just for white people. Tired rhetoric about the sanctity of *individual rights* is not enough to silence the demand for *group* rights; smarter thinkers find a way to fuse the two. The old defenders of the faith are out of ideas or they have just stopped asking the right questions. But on the left there is an inability – or a refusal – to see the potential of liberalism. They dismiss it with empty slogans about 'dead white men'. The truth is, as French philosopher Pascal Bruckner, said 'western civilisation is a jailer that slips you the key'.

Treaties, constitutional recognition, can be consistent with Australia's democratic principles; indeed, Australia would be strengthened. Rather than locked into exclusive, restrictive group identities, individuals, previously marginalised in Australia, would be freed to explore the full range of their affiliations, ambitions and desires, and identify themselves how they would wish. They could believe in an Australia that had not always believed in them.

The Uluru Statement is a high water mark in the history of Australian liberalism. It came after an exhaustive process of consultation from the top end to the Tasman Sea, from the cities to the red centre. People listened and were heard, stories were shared, and tears shed. Some have walked away and renounced it, as is their right. But at a convention at Uluru there was abiding resolve born of consensus. A people for whom Australian democracy was first designed to exclude were saying that democracy can work for them.

There are those in Australia, people with their own deep commitment to liberalism, who find fault with the Uluru Statement. They believe that race should have no place in our constitution and I agree with them. But we should remember, race is baked into our democracy. It was there at the very beginning. Section 51(xxvi) of the constitution – commonly referred to as the 'race power' – authorised the parliament to make laws for 'the people of any race, other than the aboriginal race in any state, for whom it is deemed necessary to make special laws'. It wasn't until the referendum of 1967 that the words 'other than the aboriginal race' were deleted.

The referendum also struck out section 127, that had said, 'In reckoning the numbers of the people of the Commonwealth … aboriginal natives shall not be counted.' Yet section 25 remains, allowing for the disqualification from voting of persons of any race.

By now we should have moved beyond the scientifically discredited and destructive ideas of race. Race should have no place in our constitution. But Indigenous peoples are not a race, they are the First Peoples of a land; in some parts of the world there are Indigenous people who would be classified as 'white'. The Uluru Statement does not seek a voice for a race, but representation for a people. They are a people for whom the federal government can still make special laws, they are a people for whom our courts recognise unique rights such as native title, they are a people who have endured a history, at times, of neglect, segregation and discrimination.

Democracy's strength is its capacity for innovation and self-correction. In many parts of the world democracies recognise and incorporate rights and laws framed around difference. Canada allows for the cultural autonomy of Quebec, and its Canadian Charter of Rights and Freedoms extends a constitutional protection of language groups. In Canada, collective and individual rights coexist. The Uluru Statement makes a plea to empower the powerless here and ignite the individual potential of each Indigenous person in Australia. As the statement says:

> When we have power over our destiny our children will
> flourish. They will walk in two worlds and their culture will
> be a gift to their country.

The Uluru Statement from the Heart asks much of us. It tests whether Australian democracy can be truly representative, hold a place for those whose numbers are so few, whose history is so unfair and whose burden is so heavy. It asks of Australia's political leaders, vision and courage. It asks much too from Indigenous people. Can we set aside historical grievance? Can we look to a civic unity with our fellow Australians, beyond our difference? The Uluru Statement includes a Yolngu word from Arnhem Land: Makarrata. It asks us all, can we make peace after our struggle?

WHAT TO US IS
26 JANUARY?

What, to the American slave, is your fourth of July? I
answer: a day that reveals to him, more than all other days
in the year, the gross injustice and cruelty to which he is the
constant victim. To him, your celebration is a sham; your
boasted liberty, an unholy license; your national greatness,
swelling vanity; your sounds of rejoicing are empty and
heartless; your denunciations of tyrants, brass fronted
impudence; your shouts of liberty and equality, hollow
mockery; your prayers and hymns, your sermons and
thanksgivings, with all your religious parade, and
solemnity, are, to him, mere bombast, fraud, deception,
impiety, and hypocrisy – a thin veil to cover up crimes
which would disgrace a nation of savages. There is not a
nation on the earth guilty of practices, more shocking and
bloody, than are the people of these United States, at this
very hour.

Go where you may, search where you will, roam
through all the monarchies and despotisms of the old
world, travel through South America, search out every
abuse, and when you have found the last, lay your facts by

> the side of the everyday practices of this nation, and you
> will say with me, that, for revolting barbarity and shameless
> hypocrisy, America reigns without a rival.

Frederick Douglass was born in 1818, his mother a slave and his father most likely the white man who administered the Maryland plantation his family was held on. As a boy he was considered so insolent he was sent away to be 'broken' by a cruel overseer in a property reserved for troublesome slaves. He was made to work from dawn to dark and was beaten almost daily. By the time he died he was one of the most famous men in America, a confidant of the rich and powerful, an intellectual, a writer and a devastating speaker. In 1852, a decade before the Civil War, Douglass gave a speech 'What to the Slave is the Fourth of July?'. It was a fiery denunciation of America, an America that denied its own creed of equality even as it celebrated the date of the nation's birth. But there was something else here, a profound belief in the hope of America. The hope lay in the constitution, what Douglass called a 'glorious document'. If America lived up to the full measure of its constitution, he believed, it would set all people free. As Douglass wrote, 'I do not despair of this country', within the constitution was salvation, a document he said was, 'entirely hostile to the existence of slavery'. As he wrote, 'The arm of the Lord is not shortened, and the doom of slavery is certain.'

I look to Frederick Douglass and ask the same question here: What to the Aborigine is 26 January? It is a question that Indigenous people have long posed. There are echoes of Douglass in the Day of Mourning, 26 January 1938. On the 150th anniversary of colonisation the Aborigines Progressive Association organised a protest march through the streets of

Sydney. They were turned away from Sydney Town Hall and held a meeting instead at the Australian Hall, but were told they could enter only by the back door. A hundred people turned out, among them members of my own family, in what is considered one of the first civil rights gatherings. They delivered a manifesto declaring that 'This festival of 150 years so-called "progress" in Australia commemorates also 150 years of misery and degradation imposed on the original native inhabitants by white invaders of this country.' The meeting concluded with a resolution that stated:

> WE, representing THE ABORIGINES OF AUSTRALIA,
> assembled in Conference at the Australian Hall, Sydney, on
> the 26th day of January, 1938, this being the 150th
> anniversary of the whitemen's seizure of our country,
> HEREBY MAKE PROTEST, against the callous treatment
> of our people by the whitemen during the past 150 years,
> AND WE APPEAL to the Australian nation of today to
> make new laws for the education and care of Aborigines,
> and we ask for a new policy which will raise our people to
> FULL CITIZEN STATUS and EQUALITY WITHIN THE
> COMMUNITY.

Here is a tension that exists today. A celebration of a national day that for so many of the First Peoples of this continent remains a day of pain, a reminder of a history of segregation, exclusion and brutality. But here too was a powerful statement of belief and hope in this nation. That despite our history, the promise of democracy could include even those locked out. Like Frederick Douglass, the people who met on that Day of Mourning, believed that the 'arm of the lord is not shortened', that as Martin Luther King Jnr would say decades later, 'the moral arc of the universe bends towards justice'.

26 January 2017: my father was to be awarded a special Australia Day honour in his hometown as a respected elder of his community. My father has lived a life at times at the coalface of bigotry and brutality; there have been beatings and dark nights of lockdown in a cell. He has been judged by the colour of his skin, by those who would not see the full content of his character. Yet for it all he has remained a man proud of who he is, and unwavering in his belief and hope that Australia is better than its worst. In his later years he has helped to revive his language, Wiradjuri, teaching it not just to Indigenous people but allowing all Australians to share in his heritage. Because, to my father, it is all our heritage. If you are on this land, this belongs to you. My father has been awarded an Order of Australia medal, and a doctorate from Charles Sturt University for writing the first full dictionary of Wiradjuri language.

That evening I spoke to my mother, and she told me how proud she was of how well my father was treated, and what an honour it was to celebrate on that day, when Australians celebrate all that we have made in this country. But my mother told me again of another Australia. As our conversation often does, it turned gently to her life as a young girl, living with her family, a black father and a white mother, on the outskirts of Coonabarabran in north western New South Wales. On this Australia Day she reminded me of how her family's tin humpy was bulldozed to the ground, she told me of the constant presence and threat of welfare officers, of her brothers and sisters made wards of the state and separated from their family, she told me again of seeing her father led through the streets handcuffed and roped together with other Aboriginal men, arrested for simply drinking alcohol. This is her Australia. These are her memories, the memories of wounds. We talked about Australia Day, a day that had been one of pride. 'It wouldn't hurt them to move the date,' she said.

*

Should we move the date? There are those who would abolish Australia Day entirely. They reject the very idea of Australia. In 2017 I finally had to answer this question for myself. What did I believe? I was speaking to a group of university students, touching on issues of identity and belonging and how I had lived my life to free myself from the chains of history, to move beyond narrowly defined ideas of who or what I should be. One of the students asked me what I thought about Australia Day. It is a question I have wrestled with, torn between pride in my country and my family's legacy of suffering. I could so easily have repeated that mantra that the date is offensive, a reminder of invasion and colonisation. There are times in my life when those words would have fallen easily from my lips. But I know now, we are asking ourselves the wrong question.

Australia is more than a day, it is more than a date – whatever that date may be. Moving the date or abolishing Australia Day does not answer the question, who are we? I fear moving the date would only hand it to those who would reclaim it as a day of white pride, turning it into a bombastic day of division. There are also those Indigenous people who cling to Nietzsche's 'politics of *ressentiment*', whose identities are so wedded to grievance that to relinquish their anger would be to lose their sense of themselves; moving the date would not satisfy them.

Here is the question I posed at the start of this book: on this day am I meant to be at war with myself? No. On this day I am neither black nor white, I am its synthesis: I am an Australian. That is all I can be. I am a convict in irons on a ship called *Providence*, a young Irishman banished forever from his land with no home other than the one he would make here. I am a young man not 100 years after the British boats dropped anchor, huddled in the boat shed at Circular Quay with those other survivors of the disease and violence that ravaged the first people of this land. I am John Grant and I am Frank Foster. I am the view from the ship and the view from the shore.

This is my blessing and my curse; I am blessed to be born to a nation that cherishes freedom – the freedom to rail against the nation itself, to question, to protest. In our world today that is so rare. Ours is a nation that struggles with itself, with the worst we have been, and whose arc of history has delivered us to a point where we are among the most free, prosperous and cohesive nations on earth. Yet, for all that, I am cursed to be born into the crosshairs of this nation's past; to carry that burden and see it carved into the skin and the souls of so many of my family – some of them broken by this place and others so gloriously and utterly defiant.

For me, there are the words of Albert Camus: 'Let those who want to, stand aside from the world. I no longer feel sorry for myself, for now I see myself being born.' There have been times when I have indeed felt sorry for myself; when the view from the shore was one of unceasing suffering and inevitable doom. No amount of what we would call success, of wealth or glory, could erase the pain that I have inherited. But I have a choice, to see myself as someone with a future, to believe that Australia holds a place for me too and that we can change it and that we have changed it.

The story of this country asks us to choose: what do we believe? Must I be cursed like Sisyphus, forever doomed to roll the boulder of our history to the top of the mountain only to return again to the bottom? A nation is a narrative, it is a story, it is what we imagine, it is what we choose. For me, I choose the historian, Inga Clendinnen, and the 'springtime of trust' over the anthropologist, Bill Stanner and his 'history of indifference'. Is this naive? No, it is hope. This is the hope of the storytellers who have shaped my life. As Camus wrote: 'We struggle and suffer to reconquer our solitude. But a day comes when the earth has its simple and primitive smile.'

David Malouf, the Australian poet and novelist, has called Australia an 'experiment'. 'It has taken us a long time to see it in this light', he writes, 'and even longer to accept the lightness, the freedom, the possibility that offers as a way of being'.

Think of when this thing Australia, this nation, this place, this idea was born: it is a child of upheaval and philosophy. By 1788, the United States had gone through revolution; within a year France would follow. What was it to be free? What were the rights of man? How should we be governed? These were the great questions of the age. It was a time of industrial revolution, new industries were born, global trade accelerated. My ancestors could not possibly have stood aside from this change, the world was coming, foreign ships had been circling these shores for centuries before the strangers came to stay; it would always be cataclysmic but it was not an end. I am – we all are – what came after.

Australia was part of the great Enlightenment experiment; a triumph of reason over superstition, belief in the fundamental equality of people, a rejection of *ancien regime* – of hierarchy. In his book *The Land of Dreams*, David Kemp says Australia was at the cutting edge of these ideas:

> If any society was to be based on the recognition of the equality of each individual person, Australia's historical circumstances and culture gave it the best opportunity to achieve such equality'.

Women, Catholics, Asians, Indigenous people, all have at times been excluded from this dream of Australian liberalism. But one by one the barriers have fallen, even as we reach still for the full measure of that equality.

Australia's foundations of Enlightenment and liberalism are my inheritance too. Some may think that odd. Some would argue that liberalism is the handmaiden of colonisation and oppression. It is true that some of the foundation thinkers of liberalism, some of the great Enlightenment philosophers, said horrifically racist things. But the idea is greater than those individuals. Liberalism need not exclude the aspirations of Indigenous people; a philosophy rooted in the primacy of the individual can still incorporate the rights of groups. Australia already does. British law that could be used to claim this land for the Crown could also ultimately acknowledge the claims of those whose land was taken.

I return again to that image so beloved of Inga Clendinnen – Aboriginal people and the British, dancing hand in hand on the beach. It was painted by Lieutenant William Bradley, an officer on the First Fleet, who would leave many such images depicting the early days of contact between two such different peoples. Clendinnen's is a romantic view: a dream of what could have been more than what was. Those people dancing with the white strangers would soon be ravaged by disease and violence. Clendinnen was accused of glossing over 'the wrongs of colonisation'. Others have pointed out that the same painting reveals red-coated soldiers armed, their guns at the ready. But that is Australia; it is still those who meet with open hands and those who stare with clenched fists.

I wonder now, when I write about this Australia, what others might think; how my words may so easily be hijacked by the culture warriors on all sides of politics. On the one hand there are those defenders of the empire who would brook no criticism of colonisation, who see only the benevolence of British settlement and the unquestionable glory of all that has been created here; on the other are those who see only invasion and misery, whose identity is tied to grievance. No doubt to them I would be a traitor, an 'Uncle Tom', a 'coconut'. So be it. I am not them; I don't stand apart from the world, I cannot condemn Australia without acknowledging too that I am an Australian: its failings are mine and to change it I must embrace it; embrace it all.

I think of those protesters I saw on the television in Hong Kong and the anger on their faces. I have never been one much for protests – necessary as some may be I have always been wary of the voice of the mob. Slogans always sound too harsh – too simplistic – for me. When the placards and the flags have been put away, when the streets have been cleared, how do we go forward? How do we build a country for all? Who are we? That's what I ask. For others it is, 'What side are you on?' Later that day, in a place thousands of kilometres from my homeland, I gave thanks for my country. In the acknowledgment of country I paid respects to my ancestors – those people of the first sunrise on our continent – and I spoke too of my family who came here in chains, bound to convict ships.

Where is Australia? I have looked everywhere for her. Is she in Lake Mungo, that vanishing place where time turns in on itself? Is she in the boy Bennelong standing on a rock looking out to sea, waiting for the boats with wings to return? Is she in Captain Arthur Phillip whose world was turned upside down, who lost his sense of England and yet wondered if this land would ever open to welcome him? She is in the lost girls of Hanging Rock. She is in the doomed figure of Keneally's Jimmie Blacksmith, a man caught violently between black and white. We have painted her. We have sung songs to her. We have written her. We have shed our blood on her. We have shed blood for her.

Tim Winton wrote, 'This country leans in on you. It weighs down hard, like family. To my way of thinking, it *is* family.' Yes Tim, it is. Australia is in me. I have left and returned and I am still looking.

Should we move Australia Day? Perhaps someday we will. Perhaps someday we will have settled our 'unfinished business'; but then, nations are forever unfinished; we write our stories in the margins. For now, 26 January is all that we are. It is all that we are not. Australia lives in that tension; when we seek to neutralise that tension, we deny ourselves. Some have said we should commemorate 25 and 26 January; we should mark the before and after. It is a poignant and poetic idea, but it marks an

ending and a beginning and I don't believe in that; we see what
became before and what came after. I do not exist on 25 January.
What happened on that day when the boats came to stay, that's
what has made me. I live with it all.

*

In Australia we are presented with a challenge to our nation,
one that stems from history itself. The idea of Indigenous
recognition seeks restoration in an exercise of reconciliation.
But recognition walks a national fault line: history, race. These
are things that can divide, yet cannot be ignored. Recognition
itself challenges us to make good on the past, yet live free of its
chains – to remember in order to forget. Ernest Renan told us a
nation demands it of us:

> Man is a slave neither of his race, his language, his
> religion, the course of his rivers, nor the direction of his
> mountain ranges. A great aggregation of men, in sane
> mind and warm heart, created a moral conscience that
> calls itself a nation.

Recognition is the struggle for our moral conscience. It is also a
test of how we are governed. Can our constitution satisfy the
demands of what Canadian philosopher James Tully calls our
'strange multiplicity'? Tully says we find ourselves locked in
intractable conflicts of nationalism and federalism, linguistic and
ethnic minorities, feminism and multiculturalism and the
demands of Indigenous rights. He writes: 'The question is
whether a constitution can give recognition to the legitimate

demands of the members of diverse cultures that renders everyone their due ...'

Our constitution – our founding document – must respect what came before: it must acknowledge the place of the First Peoples. Others have described it as our nation's rule book. It is a rule book that still carries the illegitimacy and stain of race, so it surely needs amendment. This land's First Peoples have felt the sting of exclusion and discrimination. It is the challenge of a nation to rise above its past. Can our constitution meet the aspirations of those locked out at the nation's birth? Will the First Peoples be given full voice to shape our destinies and complete our union with our fellow Australians?

These things need not be incompatible. The First Peoples do not have special rights, but inherent rights. It diminishes no one to acknowledge and protect that unique status, in keeping with the spirit and limits of our constitutional democracy. In this way we ensure allegiance. In this way we narrow our differences and strengthen our bonds. In this way we are all set free.

We need to write a new declaration: a Declaration of Country. It does not speak only to Indigenous people, it does not speak to Britain or the homelands of those migrants who have made their way to these shores. It speaks first to this land, this place here before any human footprint, this place that is our home.

A nation is not just a set of laws. A nation is above all a story, a never-ending story of us. It is the story of a land steeped in time, awaiting people from many other lands, who in time will call themselves Australians. It begins with the first footsteps taken tens of millennia ago, and continues in the newest-born child of this land. It will live on in those still to come. A Declaration of our Country must speak to us all. It should speak to our sense of place: our home. It should be the work of poets. It should stand alone, apart from the constitution. Its words should be carved in monuments to fall from the lips of children not yet born.

When the political debates of our age are past, there will always be our country. Our challenge – all of us – is to live here and call it home; our nation this thing of the soul.

A Declaration of Country must tell the story of Eleanor Dark's Bennilong and the story of Peter Weir's missing white girls. It must tell the story of a man called Wongamar, my Wiradjuri forebear, and the story of an Irishman, John Grant. A Declaration of Country should speak to who we have been and allow for who we may become.

*

I imagine another Australia Day, a day some time in our future when I rise at dawn and pause to remember that moment when the people of the first sunrise on this land met the people who came in the tall ships. I will fall silent for those whose lives were lost, as I do on Anzac Day and Remembrance Day. I will think of all of those who have put me here, their sacrifice, their struggles, their pain and their dreams.

I will remember, but I will also put it aside – forget if you like – for it is in forgetting that I can find peace.

This future Australia Day will still likely be a day of protest, a day of sadness, and a day of joy and thanks. We are all of those things.

On this day I will repeat to myself words I have written for my country.

The first people touched this land as our continent was being formed.
They came in boats when humanity had yet to cross an open sea.
     Here they formed a civilisation that continues to this day.
Their birthright has never been ceded.
Those people live still in their descendants.
We enter into their heritage and respect their traditions.
We honour too those who have come from other lands and carry with
     them their cultures and faiths.

Though our bonds may strain, we seek to live together in harmony.
     Though we may disagree, we find no enemy among us.

We cherish the foundations of our nation, and our rule of law and
     democracy.
We abide by the will of the majority but defend the rights of the
     minority.
We are all equal in dignity.
Opportunity is for all.
Worth should be measured not in privilege.
By our efforts we prosper. In a land of plenty, we care for those
     without.

From the first footsteps to the most recent arrival, this land is our
     home.
Here, together, we form a new people bound not by the chains of
     history but committed to a future forged together.

This is my Declaration of Country, my song of this country. For
that is what lasts.

EPILOGUE

Australia Day 2019: I was just so ineffably sad. It catches me by surprise, this sadness. I thought I no longer had it in me. I thought I had made my peace with this place; but then it hit me and I knew just where it came from; it came from memory: memory handed down, memory that is the breath of life. Just when the day was almost done, a picture-perfect day of cloudless blue sky and burning sun, my sadness overwhelmed me. I had spent the day working and then at lunch with friends at a magnificent house overlooking Sydney Harbour. They are good people, Australian people, white people – in fact, all of them white – we talked and laughed and ate and our host toasted Australia and gave thanks for the blessings of our country. I toasted Australia too, proudly. But even there surrounded by all that is good, among familiar faces, among Australians I could call my own, I felt apart.

The same thought kept returning: all of this privilege comes from loss. All of this was built on what had been taken; this country was taken and here I was among the wealthy and the good and basking in our good fortune in a land where black children still kill themselves and black mothers are beaten and black men are too often emotionally castrated, hollowed out and ground down. Then I knew, I knew that all of my efforts to understand this all; to rationalise it; to intellectualise it; all this talk of nation and forgetting and belonging and identity; all this talk about liberalism and Enlightenment; all of the books of philosophy I had studied; right there, right then it all felt so useless, so pointless, so inadequate because what had happened, here was just so, so sad.

If you are not Indigenous, it is impossible to really know what it is to carry this history in our bones, to live with the memory of wounds. I don't say that to apportion blame or shame. I love Australia and I love Australians and I am Australian but there's still that bit of me that can't truly cross the river, that lives on the other side in a bark gunyah around a fire, looking up at old stars and hearing ancient chants. I can't shake this; I am Wiradjuri, I am Kamilaroi; I come from this land; my ancestors called this their home; all of their stories, all of their songs, their art, it was all created here; they drew life from this soil. This was never empty – terra nullius was the lie that haunts us still. This is what puts people on the streets; this is where that anger comes from.

I don't share that anger anymore – that is gone and I am better for it. But sadness, deep, enduring sadness like a chasm in my soul: that I fear will never, never leave me.

I walked through the centre of Sydney and I saw people in T-shirts that said 'survival', 'invasion', that reminded passers-by that 'white Australia has a black history'; I locked eyes with these people and I knew – instinctively and profoundly – that I belonged. They were making their way back from protests and a festival that celebrated not Australia, but our endurance, our resilience and our pride. We smiled as we passed each other, the easy nod of recognition, a look that says, yes I know you. It is a look I can find nowhere else on earth; it is a look that says, 'come home brother'; it is a look that pulls me in and tells me that among these people I am safe. In their eyes I saw what I felt; I saw sadness, a look of people who have been so terribly hurt and have nothing left with which to strike back.

In their faces I saw something that I don't want to see but something I cannot deny; we are still strangers here. That space between the ship and the shore; that space where my ancestors black and white met; that space we still can't quite fill. We can love in that space; we can talk and we can dance and we can laugh; and maybe that space is big enough to hold a nation. If we are smart enough and generous enough and forgiving enough we can write our laws and our stories and we can make a place of peace there in the space between us. But we cannot squeeze 65,000 years into two hundred; time hasn't worked its healing yet.

Maybe at some time – some time so far away – when my bones are as old as the bones of Lake Mungo none of this will matter; someone will dig me up and wonder who it was that lived here.

ACKNOWLEDGEMENTS

This book is about my journey into my country and it would not have been possible without those I have shared the journey with. I want to thank my grandparents, my parents, my siblings, my uncles and aunties and cousins who have all walked this road together. My dear lifelong mate Richard 'Ditchie' Bamblett – it has been a long way from school in Griffith and you're still doing heroic work for our people. Marcia Langton, thank you for lighting a fire in my mind and inspiring me still. Noel Pearson, Megan Davis, Pat Anderson: what warriors you are. Hugh Riminton, John Vause, Farhad Shadravan, Brad Olson, Steve Jiang, Tim Schwarz, my compadres on the adventure of journalism. Peter Ford, thanks for our conversations. Richard Flanagan, the writer I wish to be. Mark Bannerman, my friend and soul brother, thanks for opening up a world of music and words for me. As always my deep gratitude and thanks to all HarperCollins, my editor Nicola Robinson who made this a better book, Tara Wynne my agent and the team at Curtis Brown. To Tracey, my love and my life, and my children, my love and my hope.

SELECTED SOURCES

Kwame Anthony Appiah, *The Ethics of Identity*, Princeton University Press, Princeton, 2007.

Thomas Brudholm, *Resentment's Virtue: Jean Amery and the Refusal to Forgive*, Temple University Press, Philadelphia, 2008.

Andrew S. Curran, *The Anatomy of Blackness: Science and Slavery in the Age of Enlightenment*, John Hopkins University Press, Baltimore, 2011.

Eleanor Dark, *The Timeless Land*, Macmillan, Sydney, 1941.

Megan Davis & Marcia Langton (Ed.), *It's Our Country: Indigenous Arguments for Meaningful Constitutional Recognition and Reform*, Melbourne University Press, Melbourne, 2016.

W.E.B. Du Bois, *The Souls of Black Folk*, Restless Books, New York City, 2017.

Catriona Elder, *Being Australian: Narratives of National Identity*, Allen and Unwin, Sydney, 2007.

Edmund Fawcett, *Liberalism – The Life of an Idea*, Princeton University Press, Princeton, 2018.

Vincenzo Ferrone, *The Enlightenment: History of an Idea*, Princeton University Press, Princeton, 2015.

Barbara J. Fields & Karen Elsie Fields, *Racecraft – The Soul of Inequality in American Life*, Verso, New York City, 2014.

Francis Fukuyama, *The End of History and the Last Man*, Free Press, New York City, 1992.

Ken Gelder & Jane M. Jacobs, *Uncanny Australia*, Melbourne University Press, Melbourne, 1994.

Sue Grand & Jill Salberg (Ed.), *The Wounds of History – Repair and Resilience in the Trans-Generational Transmission of Trauma*, Routledge, Abingdon, 2017.

Stan Grant, *The Australian Dream: Blood, History and Becoming*, Quarterly Essay Issue 64, Black Inc, Melbourne, 2016.

John N. Gray, *Enlightenment's Wake*, Routledge, Abingdon, 1995.

Gertrude Himmelfarb, *The Roads to Modernity*, Vintage Books, New York City, 2008.

Duncan Ivison, *Postcolonial Liberalism*, Cambridge University Press, Cambridge, 2002.

Duncan Ivison, Paul Patton & Will Sanders, *Political Theory and the Rights of Indigenous Peoples*, Cambridge University Press, Cambridge, 2000.

Karl Jaspers, *Nietzsche – An Introduction to the Understanding of his Philosophical Activity*, John Hopkins University Press, Baltimore, 1997.

Elliot L. Jurist, *Beyond Hegel and Nietzsche*, The MIT Press, Cambridge, 2000.

Will Kymlicka, *Multicultural Citizenship: A Liberal Theory of Minority Rights*, Oxford University Press, Oxford, 1995.

Mark Lilla, *The Once and Future Liberal: After Identity Politics*, HarperCollins, New York City, 2017.

Mark Lilla, *The Shipwrecked Mind: On Political Reaction*, New York Review of Books, New York City, 2016.

Charles W. Mills, *Black Rights/White Wrongs: A Critique of Racial Liberalism*, Oxford University Press, Oxford, 2017.

Czeslaw Milosz, *The Captive Mind*, Alfred A. Knopf, New York City, 1953.

Nicolas Peterson & Will Sanders (Ed.), *Citizenship and Indigenous Australians: Changing Conceptions and Possibilities*, Cambridge University Press, Cambridge, 1998.

Terry Pinkard, *Does History Make Sense?*, Harvard University Press, Cambridge, 2017.

Elizabeth Povinelli, *The Cunning of Recognition*, Duke University Press, Durham, 2002.

John Rawls, *A Theory of Justice*, Harvard University Press, Cambridge, 1999.

Paul Ricoeur, *Memory, History, Forgetting*, University of Chicago Press, Chicago, 2004.

David Rieff, *In Praise of Forgetting: Historical Memory and Its Ironies*, Yale University Press, New Haven, 2016.

Tommie Shelby, *We Who are Dark*, Harvard University Press, Cambridge, 2005.

Steven B. Smith, *Modernity and Its Discontents*, Yale University Press, New Haven, 2016.

Elspeth Tilley, *White Vanishing: Rethinking Australia's Lost-in-the-Bush Myth*, Rodopi, Amsterdam, 2012.

David Tracey, *Edge of the Sacred*, HarperCollins, Sydney, 1995.

Hayden White, *Metahistory: The Historical Imagination in Nineteenth Century Europe*, John Hopkins University Press, Baltimore, 1973.

Patrick Wolfe, *Traces of History: Elementary Structures of Race*, Verso, New York City, 2016.

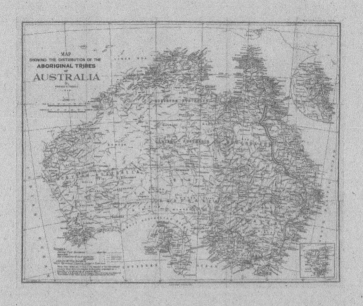

The cover of this book shows a section of anthropologist and ethnologist Norman Tindale's map of Aboriginal group boundaries, which was published in 1974, the result of 50 years' research. When Tindale began his mapping project in the 1920s, the official orthodoxy was that Aboriginal people roamed across the landscape, with no connection to specific regions. Although Tindale's methodology has been superseded and the map itself is imperfect, it remains an important document in Australian history – visible evidence that no part of the continent was terra nullius, empty land.

STAN GRANT

talking to my country

'A story so essential and salutary to this place that it should be given out free at the ballot box' Sydney Morning Herald

TALKING TO MY COUNTRY

Talking to My Country is Stan Grant's very personal meditation on race, identity and history. It is that rare and special book that talks to every Australian about their country – what it is, and what it could be. It is not just about race, or about Indigenous people but all of us, our shared identity. Direct, honest and forthright, Stan is talking to us all. He might not have all the answers but he wants us to keep on asking the question: how can we be better?

'an urgent and flowing narrative in a book that should be on the required reading list in every school' – *The Australian*

'Grant will be an important voice in shaping this nation' – *The Saturday Paper*

'A story so essential and salutary to this place that it should be given out free at the ballot box' – *The Sydney Morning Herald*

a family memoir

The Tears of Strangers

STAN GRANT

'a moving story'
Sydney Morning Herald